HISTORICAL STUDIES ON GLOBAL SCAM AND NIGERIA'S 419

HOW TO OVERCOME FRAUDSTERS AND CON ARTISTS

Tunde Akingbade

authorHOUSE®

AuthorHouse™
1663 Liberty Drive
Bloomington, IN 47403
www.authorhouse.com
Phone: 1-800-839-8640

First published by AuthorHouse 5/1/2009

ISBN: 978-1-4389-7596-2 (sc)

Printed in the United States of America
Bloomington, Indiana

This book is printed on acid-free paper.

Dedication

To late Pa Philip Adeyemo Oketola and late Madam
Victoria Abebi Oketola.

You tief one kobo dey put you for prison,
You tief ten million, na patriotism,
Den go give you chieftaincy and national honour.
You tief even bigger den go say na rumour
Monkey dey work, baboon dey chop
Sweet pounded yam–some day e go stop!*

Wole Soyinka,
Nobel Prize Winner, 1986

*If you steal one kobo they will put you in prison
But if you still ten million, they will say its patriotism
Even if you still bigger they will tell us it's a rumour
While monkey is working, baboon is eating
The sweet pounded yam and all this nonsense will stop some day

From the lyrics of Unlimited Liability Company, 1983

Contents

PREFACE

Historically, one can trace the root of all deception to the Garden of Eden when Satan was said to have gone to deceive Eve by persuading her to eat the fruit which God forbade her and Adam from eating. From that moment onwards, one could aptly say that a chain of deception commenced. Eve in turn, persuaded Adam to have a bite of the fruit.

Today, deception has wept across the world on a large and unimaginable scale. All through Biblical times, deception took a toll on the human race.

A cursory look at the evolution and development of countries in Europe and America will reveal deception of a particular race or group of people at the foundation of the modern powers that control the economies of the world. Deception too is at the base of the relationship between the Western world and Africa in pre-colonial, colonial and post colonial eras. Walter Rodney, the world's renowned scholar and author of *How Europe Under Developed Africa* indicated in his epic work that "it is absolutely necessary to determine whether the standard of living in a given industrialized country is a product of its own internal resources or whether it stems from exploiting other countries "adding that" the United States has a small proportion of the word's population and exploitable natural wealth but it enjoys a huge percentage of the wealth which comes from exploiting the labour and natural resources of the whole world." That was Rodney's impression of the last millennium. Regrettably; the events of those centuries have laid the foundational or generational problems on Africa in the 21st Century.

Professor Howard Zinn, author of *A People's History of the United States* writes in his book about how some big names in the country used stealing and deception to reap from unsuspecting people. Zinn who I once spoke with on *VOA's Talk to America* programme indicates in his book how some rich Americans as far back as the 19th Century bribed the legislature to legalize their shady deals.

J.P Morgan, the son of a banker for example, Zinn notes under "Robbers, Barons and Rebels" that during the American civil war, bought 5,000 rifles for $3.50 each from an army arsenal and sold them to a general in the field for $22 each. These rifles were found to be defective and they would shoot off the thumb of the soldiers using them.

"A congressional committee noted this in the small print of the obscure report, but a Federal judge upheld the deal as a fulfillment of a valid legal contact," Professor Zinn adds.

It is gratifying to note that there were, and there are some good Nigerians in spite of the primitive greed and deception in the country in and out of government.

Justice Emmanuel Ayoola, Chairman of Independent Corrupt Practices and other offences Commission, (ICPC) recalled in *The News* magazine edition of August 25, 2008 that its puzzling how the Nigerian society moved from the path of integrity very swiftly over the years to a society where "convicted people are received with drums and music and they go to Church for thanksgiving" adding that "sometimes, the Pastor even rain curses on the people who send them to jail."

This is a country that the level of corruption would have made people to forget that a one-time military governor, Adekunle Fajuyi was once offered bribe by a Briton in 1996. Sami Ajiki Fajuyi's biographer recalls in his book how Fajuyi called the Head of Civil Service and requested that the bribe be paid into government treasury, to the people's coffers! General Ironsi, Nigeria's first military ruler died without leaving anything for his family. Nigeria's first Prime Minister Sir Abulbakar Tafawa Balewa, Sir Ahmadu Bello, Premier of the North, Chief Obafemi Awolowo and Dr. Nnamdi Azikiwe did not accumulate wealth with the senseless greed that we now see in the country. They left a legacy in all sectors of the economy despite their political differences.

It should be noted also that when Nigeria's economy was booming and the naira had higher value, people were more honest, although poverty is not an excuse to be devilish in quest for material things.

Africa's human and natural resources have been exploited at an alarming rate through Trans Sahara and Trans Atlantic Slave trade. This inhuman trade also had deception as the underlying factors that made it easy to subjugate Africans. Even on the eve of colonial disengagement from Africa, the colonial powers used deception, divide and rule tactics on the new Africa leaders. Even during and after the era of military *coup de tats,* the colonial powers still pull strings using deception and connivance with African rulers to further subjugate the people, rendering them poor. Most African leaders and imperialist's agent took their stolen wealth to the West. The resultant effect has been a continent of millions of people wallowing in abject poverty and unemployment. Just as it was in the last millennium, Africans are still moving in droves to develop other continents and scheming at the same time to survive at home under desperate and criminal guises.

It is instructive to note that institutional deception in Nigeria, over the years, for example, is one of the cardinal reasons for the development of the shameful private deception and crime of persuasion industry or scam where individuals have stolen money from people and organizations around the world. This book is an insight into the evolution of scam in Nigeria and its global significance.

The Nigerian society under the current democratic dispensation since 1999 when the military was shown the exit from political office has been strange. Many strange and deceitful things are happening in government, compounding the problems of the governed. Think about this. The democratically elected government under former President Olusegun Obasanjo said that his government subsidized petroleum price usage in our oil producing nation. But renowned economist, Professor Sam Aluko said this was not true and that from available records government subsidized nothing!

It is pertinent to mention that in recent times, institutionalized deception plays a very important role in the life of an average Nigerian leading to the criminal and desperate move to survive. For example, how do you explain a democratic government who claimed that petroleum was subsidized, yet the same government jerked up the pump prices of petroleum products while people were sleeping?

Can we claim that such a government was different from a military regime who under the guise of structural adjustment imposed by the Western economists devalued Nigeria's currency while the nation was asleep, and laid the foundation of Nigeria's economic retrogression and loss of ethics and values in the past two decades?

The contributions of Professors Mobolaji Aluko and Okey Ndibe through various articles in exposing deception in all its ramifications are hereby acknowledged. I have been investigating cases of scam as a journalist since 1996 and this book contains some of my findings and publications. I also acknowledge the use of materials by several experts, writers, the internet, known and unknown artists in the making of the book. It is pertinent to mention that operators of the deception industry are often intoxicated by wine of deceit that they do not differentiate between the names of Nigerians in Diaspora and foreigners in their craze for hard currency.

In between these, the Economic and Financial Crimes Commission and the Independent Corrupt Practices Commission (ICPC) have taken some corrupt persons to court for embezzlement and some have begun to succumb to pressure promising they will return their loot! No matter their hurdles and set backs, we should give kudos to the effort of the EFCC once led by Mallam Nuhu Ribadu and now Mrs. Farida Waziri and the Independent Corrupt Practices Commission(ICPC) for at list giving a ray of hope. Professor Mrs. Dora Akunyili of NAFDAC equally falls within the bracket of a new generation of persons that have given a positive direction in a disgusting and rotten system that has mesmerized a whole generation of people and their international conspirators into deception and corruption.

I am grateful to all those who through interactions have one way or the other contributed to my career in writing and investigative journalism. Many thanks to Jahman Anikulapo, Editor, *The Guardian on Sunday*, Bayo Ogunmupe, Emmanuel Mayah, Emmanuel France,

Tosan Roro-Ogoshe. Mr. Soji Omotunde, General Manager, *The Nation*, Mr. Segun Adeniyi, Media Adviser to the President, Prof. H. Inyang, Duke Energy Distinguished Professor, UNCC, USA, Dr. Victor Fodeke, Mr. Tunde Fodeke UNCC, USA, for every recognition accorded me.

In recent times, Mr. Kunle Oyatomi, Editor *Sunday Vanguard* has been of immense inspiration. There are other colleagues in the media such as Shola Oshunkeye, *CNN/Multichoice* Journalist of the year 2006, Femi Adesina, Executive Director, *Sun*, Louis Odion, Editor, *National Daily*, Basil Okafor and Pastor Tayo Agboola who found this work interesting.

It is pertinent to mention that my interaction and recognition from various people helped to shape my world outlook. They include; Chief Duro Onabule Dele Momodu, *Ovation International* Deji Aiyelabowo, Shola Aiyelabola, AIT, Lagos, Mr. Peter Igho, Mr. Ray Yusuf, Alhaji Adetunji Majeed, Mrs. Antoinette Falohun of Nigeria Television Authority.

Thanks to my friends, in Berlin, Amsterdam and USA, Peter Prufert, Marco Van Kerkhoven, Leigh Herrick, Branko Gulin, Nicole Peskin, Susan Sakash and Alex Primm. I appreciate Uncle Isaiah Oketola, Uncle Moses Oketola, Dr. D. Oyinloye, Dr. Gboyega Macaulay, Mr. Ayo Da Silva, PDP Senatorial Candidate, Lagos West, Nosa Osazuwa, United Nations Information Centre, Lagos, Stephen Ogundijo, Sola Ayo Aderele, nee Fakoya, Dr and Mrs. Nath Ayo Macaulay, Mr. and Mrs. J.B. Macaulay, Mr. and Mrs. Yemi Oketola

Dr. & Mrs. Otegbeye, Ambassador Segun Olusola, Mr. & Mrs. Jide Fasoyin, Dr. Dotun Malomo, Special Adviser for Health, Ogun State government, Mr. Oladipo Bali, Dr. Ola Balogun Mr. Sola Balogun Art Editor, *Sun*, Makin Soyinka. In everything I do, I cannot forget Professor Siyan Oyeweso, Lagos State University (LASU), Professor Richard Olaniyan Obafemi Awolowo University, Ile-Ife, Professor Tunde Babawale, Funmi Adewunmi, UNILAG, Mr. Femi Falana, Professor Dipo Kolawole, Vice Chancellor, University of Ado Ekiti, Professor Bayo Lawal, former Head of Department of History, University of Lagos, Richard Akinnola, Femi Ojudu, Kunle Ajibade, Mr. Seye Kehinde of *City People Magazine*, Senator Tokunbo Afikuyomi, Commissoner for Tourism, Lagos State, Mr. Kabir, *The Guardian*, Mr. Sam Otoo, Mr. Ganiyu Omolade, Mr. Tony Ofoyetan, Otunba Femi Oduntan, member of IVP Alumni Association of US embassy, Femi Omowunmi, Joke Omotunde of PAS, Mike Awoyinfa, Pastors Kunle Macualay, Laide Sokunbi, Biodun Denloye. There are several others I cannot mention.

The programmes and commentaries of presenters such as; Charles Anasodo, Cordelia Ogbe, *Radio Nigeria*, Mrs. Ibiyemi Ajadi, *Paramount FM*, kept me on through the lonely days and nights working on the scripts. Akindeji and Akintude Akingbade are wonderful boys. Above all, I thank God for making this possible.

Tunde Akingbade.

CHAPTER ONE

Nigerian's Political Crisis and Genesis of Deception in the Country

The British Colonial government amalgamated the northern and southern protectorates of Nigeria in 1914 under Sir Fredrick Lugard. The entire landmass of the country is made up of about 250 ethnic groups and three main tribes, the Hausa in the North, Yoruba in the West and Ibo in the East.

The British administrative style caused problem in many parts of the country. In the North, they imposed the indirect rule system by which they ruled through the Emirs who were acceptable to the people. They also succeeded in the West where traditional institutions also flourished and was respected but they failed in the East because there were no such structures. They therefore imposed what was called "warrant chiefs" which were not accepted by the people.

British interest in Nigeria was purely economic.

(See Chapter Two, How the British Taught Nigerians How To Steal).

However, following the World War II, there were agitations for independence from British. Sir Arthur Richards (later Lord Millverton) who was the Governor General of Nigeria created a constitution (Richard's Constitution in 1947). Some historians have argued that this constitution "was a bad start" for Nigeria because as Fredrick Forsyth the renowned British author argued in one of his works, from a unitary state, ruled by a central legislative authority, Nigeria became a three-region Federal State in 1947. There were many regional conferences during the period and the North was allocated more seats than the rest of the country. Then some Northern politicians argued for a loose federation and that the amalgamation of the North and South was a mistake.

There was another conference in 1953 which produced another constitution. Three major political parties emerged and slugged it out among themselves to take over power from the British. The Northern People's Congress (NPC) represented the North (with Sir Ahmadu Bello as the leader), the West had the Action Group (AG) party (with Obafemi Awolowo as the leader) Citizens (NCNC) headed by Dr. Nnamdi Azikwe. After 1959 elections, the NPC and NCNC went into a coalition which made them to form the government. Sir Ahmadu Bello sent his deputy, Sir Abubakar Tafawa Balewa to head the government while Dr. Nnamdi Azikiwe became a ceremonial president. Within a year after independence, the AG broke into two factions. While Awolowo and his sympathizers were being investigated by inquiries set up by teh government at the centre, Akintola's government and their allies in the West favoured a romance with the NPC in the North. But the coalition was resented vehemently by people in the West.

In 1963, the federal government created Mid-Western Region out of the Western Region. This was thought to be a further fragmentation of the West while the huge Northern land mass remained indivisible despite the fact that the call for a Middle Belt State by the United Middle Belt Congress (Party)-made up of Tivs was rejected. There were also riots and agitations in the region contributing to the instability in the country. In 1964, there was another election.

The NPC broke her alliance with NCNC and teamed up with Akintola's faction of AG to form Nigeria Northern Alliance (NNA). The NCNC thus joined the other faction of Action Group and they formed the United Progressive Grand Alliance (UPGA)

During the 1994 election, disappearance of party officials, electoral officials, ballot boxes, detention of candidates and setting of people and homes ablaze became the order of the day. These disturbances grew in the West until the army struck on January 15, 1966.

GENESIS OF THE CIVIL WAR

The coup of January 15, 1996 was led by Major Chukwuma Kaduna Nzeogwu. He was amongst the five majors who broke the political virginity of the Nigerian Army. Others plotters were; Major Emmanuel Ifeajuna (an Ibo) Major David Okafor (an Ibo) Major Adewale Ademoyega (a Yoruba) Although Nzeogwu was (Ika) Ibo, he grew up and lived in the North during his lifetime.

Nzeogwu with a group of soldiers under the code name "Operation Danisa" forced their ways into the home of Sir Ahmadu Bello, Premier of the North in Kaduna. They killed some of the guards, some members of his household before finally killing him. It was in Kaduna that Brigadier Ademulegun and his wife were killed Shodehinde. The coup plotters in Lagos who were led by Major Ifeajuna killed the Primer Minister, Alhaji Abubakar Tafawa Balawa and minister for finance, Chief Festus Okotie-Eboh (a Mid Westerner). The soldiers also killed Brigadier Maimalari (a Northerner), Lieutenant Colonel Pam, (a northern), Lieutenant Colonel Largema. They also killed Chief S.L. Akintola and arrested his deputy, Remi Fani-Kayode who was later released. But the coup failed. Nzeogwu was dumped into detention by Major General JTU Aguiyi Ironsi (an Ibo who had a Sierra Leonean lineage). Ironsi was the head of the army. Between 1961 and 1962 when the Nigeria political crisis was talking its roots, he was military Adviser to the Nigeria High Commission in UK. Ironsi took over the reign of government when the coup failed. He came up with the so-called Unification policy to break away from regionalism which he felt led to the down fall of the politicians. But this policy did not go down well with Northern leaders the loss of their leaders to the coup. Ironsi on May 21 announced a decree called constitution (suspension and modification decree) which amongst others abolished the four regions.

Nigeria was to be a Federal Republic and not a federation. The decree sparked off riots amongst students in Kano and later engulfed the North. Throughout the North, there was a clarion call for secession. Most Ibos ran for their dear lives. Ironsi then had a tour around the country to explain his government policy. He toured the East and the

North without any hitch until he got to Ibadan. It was there on July 29, another coup led by Murtala Muhammed was carried out. Ironsi was arrested by Major .Y. Danjuma with his host, Lt. Col Adekunle Fajuyi who insisted on following his Commander-in-Chief. Both men and other were murdered. Lt. Col, Yakubu Gowon was elevated to Ironsi's post. But Ojukwu insisted that the order of seniority must be followed. The next person was Brigadier Babafemi Ogundipe (a Yoruba) and Ojukwu insisted he should be the head of the Army. But Ogundipe bolted away to London when junior officers from the North refused to take his orders. Tension and killings increased in the land and the quarrel between Ojukwu and Gowon snow balled into the Nigerian civil war.

POLITICAL 419 (DECEPTION) AND JUNE 12 ELECTIONS

Politics, according to the Oxford English Dictionary "is a dirty business"

The political terrain in Nigeria since independence on October 1, 1960 has not been clean. The political landscape has become dirtier since the Military incursion into politics on January 15, 1966.

Nigeria has had its fair share of Military coups. These coups were products of rivalry amongst the political class, and soldiers who were politicians in uniform. There were some levels of corruption and deception by the politicians in the First Republic.

However, the military, which took over from them, was composed of individuals who also messed the economy.

Below are some intriguing stories of corruption and deception, after Nigeria's independence.

In the early years of the Nigerian State, the Nigeria army has been known to have a better reputation or honesty and far from corruption than the police. The Inspector General of Police, according to N.J. Miners in his book on the *Nigerian Army 1956-66*, set up an X-squad to curb bribery in the police in 1963.

Miner noted that even in the Army, some recruits offered bribes to be accepted. One Lt. Okafor was reportedly sentenced to two years' imprisonment for stealing $2,500 from the unit's account.

He recalled how an army officer, Lt. Col. Imo was court-marshaled in 1964 "for acquiring property worth 96 pounds from the Army Ordinance Depot and for misusing army transport. *Daily Express* noted that three naval officers were dismissed in 964 for stealing $60,000 belonging to the Navy. That was almost 10 percent of naval budget at that time.

Odofin Bello, a Commissioner of Police was convicted on charges of corruption in 1966. The Treasurer of NNDP gave evidence that he paid $5,000 to Odofin Bello before the 1964 elections on the instruction of Chief S.L. Akintola. The verdict was later reversed on appeal after the July 29, 1966 Coup de tat. Before then, there was the Coker Commission of enquiry which investigated some activities of the Action Group Party.

Dr. Obarogie Ohonbamu, author of *Nigeria, the Army and the Renegades Cause* (1966) under the controversial circumstances also accused Gen. Murtala Muhammed of corruption. However, corruption and misuse of state money was frowned at in early post independence era.

CORRUPTION AND 419

Corruption has been fingered as one of the problems confronting Nigeria's leadership since independence. Virtually all the governments that came to power have been accused of corruption and diversion of public funds. Large sums of money meant for education, health and rural and urban development are known to have been stolen, diverted, kept in foreign or Swiss Bank accounts and now laundered by government officials and private collaborators at the expense of the populace. The resultant effect is the creation of an army of jobless youths and unpaid pensioners. These idle minds designed all kinds of satanic deceptions to make money and reap where they did not sow at an alarming and frightening level.

THE MILITARY

During the First Republic, the politicians were accused by the military of corruption. However, the twelve governors appointed by the military government of General Yakubu Gowon were accused of corruption of General Yakubu Gowon were also accused of corruption. A commission set up to probe the governors found only two of them not guilty of corruption. Even some of the assets of the remaining two governors were seized.

Governors U.J Esuene, of South Eastern State in Gowon's government was asked to refund N25, 672 to the coffers of the government. That was a lot of money in those days. All the ten governors found guilty in the toppled government were asked to refund a total of N3 million, which was very substantial.

The military government and the governors who were toppled on July 29, 1975 by the Gen Murtala Muhammed and Gen. Olusegun Obasanjo's government were always traveling overseas and spending recklessly. The NPN civilian government of Alhaji Shehu Shagari was worse. Many Nigerians still hold the view that the election that brought President Shagari to power with the use of "mathematics of 12 two thirds of 19 states was controversial and laced with deception-even though it got a legal backing.

The governor under the NPN controlled civilian and UPN governments were thrown into jail and accused of theft and diversion of public fund to the party at the detriment of the poor masses. A single governor or government official in the NPN government was known to have stolen more than what was stolen by all the politicians in the First Republic.

General Sani Abacha, who accused the civilians of plundering the treasury, announced the coup that brought General M. Buhari. Ironically, when Abacha himself came to power, he stashed million of dollars belonging to the country into virtually all known capitals in Europe. He committed atrocities worse than he accused his predecessors of committing Gradually, Nigeria economy collapsed. Many people fled the country and escaped from excruciating poverty and idleness at home or diverted their brains and attention to hitherto unknown fraudulent stratagem to make money. It is part of the leadership deception that made three past military Heads of State to declare at the tenth year anniversary of the demise of General Abacha that he was innocent of the cases of diversion of public funds in to personal overseas when it was actually one of them that signed the government gazette ten years earlier confirming the amount of money diverted and recovered from the various accounts. Dr. Dele Sobowale, a columnist with the *Sunday Vanguard* reminded Nigerians in his column on August 22, 2008 that it was General Abubakar who signed the Decree 35 of 1999 which forfeited the allegedly stolen assets and wealth of General Sanni Abacha. Amongst the loot forfeited to the Nigerian government was a 30 per cent share in West African Petroleum Refinery in Sierra Leone which was bought under the name Nastume Investment Limited. What was recovered from Abacha at that period was close to N600 billion. When ex-President Obasanjo came, he went on aggressive debt recovery drive and sent emissaries all over the world, including Switzerland to recover what was stolen by the ex-military leader from Nigeria. Millions of dollars were recovered by a school of thought believed that the money was subsequently filtered away in another round of ground scale fraud and deception. The Senate and House of Representatives Committee under the administration of President Umaru Yar' Adua set up robes into the power sector of the country and unearthed massive fraud which startled Nigerians about the genuineness of the Obasanjo administration while in power. Some of the aides of the former President were said to have been involved in dirty schemes and deals including acquisition of other people's houses and legalizing such immoral deals. The ex-President's daughter was also docked for allegedly being involved in the use of a fund belonging to a Ministry despite the fact that there was a Presidential order to return the fund to the coffers of the government.

JUNE 12 ELECTION AND DECEPTION

A school of through has argued vociferously that the regime of Military President, General Ibrahim Babangida (rtd) brought about the art of deception in governance in the country. Chief O.A. Rawane, once a staunch member of Action Group belonged to this school. In various articles, Rewane accused Babangida of introducing what was known as "settlement syndrome" into governance. This was a process of sealing, blocking or shutting the mouths of political opponents with money. Others argue to the contrary, however, it will be recalled that between 1989 and 1992, Babangida set in motion of a political programme which was said to be founded on a platform of deception. His critics based this on the premise that he asked politicians to form political parties, which he dissolved, and claimed many of them had no qualities to merit being registered. They claimed he knew what he wanted, yet sent politicians on wild goose chase. Then he set up his own "brand new" political parties and asked politicians to join. They did and subsequently campaigned for the presidential elections on June 12, 1993.

Babangida and his military officers later annulled the election after taking the nation on a tortuous and arduous road to election. The annulment led to riots. Gradually, the populace thought that annulling a free and fair election by IBB was unfair and that they had been taken for a ride in his grand deception.

Millions of naira was wasted on an election that took no one anywhere. This steadily gave birth to the notorious Abacha military regime.

ABACHA'S GRAND DECEPTION

It was this deception that gave birth to the interim Government, which was later thrown by General Abacha.

Abacha was believed to have surrounded himself with charlatans and those who were far from being sincere.

Did not only deceived him that he can rule for life, the regime also looked the other way as" regiments of young, educated, middle and fraudulent business persons emerged in the newly born scam industry which perfected the use of fax machine and telephone to defraud foreigners. In his grand design to rule for life, Abacha officially encouraged a national deception and amnesia known as "One Million

March" to support his regime. Despite the fact that Abacha and his goons knew that those who wanted him in power may not be up to that, they funded the recruitment of young marchers all over the country through an arrow head called Daniel Kanu.

The PDP civilian government of President Olusegun Obasanjo made so much money from oil. It made giant economic strikes, yet the government was known to have through some elected persons harboured an army of corrupt officials, politicians, unemployed youths and unpaid senior citizens and bad road networks. People engaged in crime of persuasion under the regime. The government set up the Economic and Financial Crimes Commission (EFCC) first led by Mallam Nuhu Ribadu and the Independent Corrupt Practices Commission, once led by Justice Mustapha Akanbi and now led Justice Emmanuel Ayoola. The two organizations are now led by Mrs. Farida Waziri and Justice Ayoola, respectively. Both organizations have worked within and outside the country to rid the polity of corrupt individuals and recover money stolen in and out of Nigeria fraudulently. They have also returned money stolen by some Nigerians to their original owners who are foreigners.

GOVERNANCE AND DECEPTION

After several years of military rule, Nigeria returned to democratic rule on May 29, 1999. There were high hopes that politicians would deliver the dividends of democracy to the people. Gradually, it became clear that some of those who got elected were money bags, men who were discredited in the failed Second Republic, those who falsified academic records and men of questionable character who have no name to protect. Some of them who stayed long in power stole as much as they wanted. They cared less about the suffering of the people and fed them with propaganda and deception while they traveled frequently abroad to have birthday ceremony of a London based Nigerian known as Terry Waya.

It was reported that few years into democracy virtually all governors in the country travelled to London to celebrate his fortieth birthday, President Olusegun Obasanjo berated these governors he tagged

"Owambe" (Party) governors. It took the creation of the Economic and Financial Crimes Commission (EFCC) to put to check the reckless of some governors. The most celebrated case of out money laundering and deception involving governor was that of Chief D.S.P Alaigmesiagha of Bayelsa State who was arrested in London for allegedly possessing one million pound in 2005. It was the same Terry Waya who paid the 500,000 pounds bail bond.

The Governor later escaped and returned to Nigeria and was impeached. Some of the Governors who were being trailed by EFCC were smart enough to cover their track. Others such as a former governor in a State could not hide his schemes and deception. Amongst the questionable poultry project where the birds were alleged to have been specially brought just to commission the project. He later got himself impeached in controversial circumstances.

It is however interesting to note that about the time of impeachment of Mr. Ayo Fayose, * Mr. Terry Waya, the London based Nigerian who got the bail bond of Governor Alameisiagba was arrested to answer questions in London over many cases of money laundering, obtaining money by false pretense, deception, fraud etc.

Mallam Nuhu Ribadu, former Chairman of the Economic and Financial Crimes Commission (EFCC) disclosed that from the commission's investigations, since 1960 when the nation got independence, the worst theft of public money took place between 1980s and 1990s. This took place by some government officials in collusion with many people through deception. Within three years of the operation of the EFCC, it has prosecuted 82 people caught in the web of 419 and recovered more than 5 billion dollars stolen through deception. It is instructive to note that the EFCC recovered 140 million dollars from a former Nigerian leader. About 400 million dollars was also recovered from a former Governor in Bayelsa State.

JUDICIAL 419

Deception also found its way into Nigeria's judicial system during the years of military rule. Decrees were rolled out sometimes without the knowledge of law officer or Attorney General of the country. Dr.

Olu Onagoruwa once denied the knowledge of certain "Monstrous decrees" promulgated by the Abacha Military government for which he was the Chief Law Officer. Under the Buhari Idiagbon military government, it was alleged that certain forms were made available through the back door by some people in the government who promulgated decree 2 and 4 to detain people at will, without questioning. It was alleged that anyone could have his/her name slotted into the form without legal process and find themselves in detention. Innocent people found themselves n detention without genuine legal documents.

The Abacha government also promulgated Decree No 14 of 1994 "which prohibits courts from ordering government to produce detained persons in courts." it is instructive to note that during the military regimes, Nigerian courts sat at unholy hours.

A detained presidential aspirant in Nigeria once got a bail when he was not in court and without the knowledge of any of his counsels. More worrisome is the believe that a person could prosecuted in court without his knowledge by individuals who would pay someone to assume his name and address and stand in the dock as the culprit. Richard Akinnola, one of Nigeria's most prominent human rights activist and judicial correspondents once reported how innocent people are being executed in some of Nigeria's prisons by people who substituted their names with that of convicted murderers or armed robbers. In his book, *Discharged and Acquitted* published in 2008 Akinnola noted that while the innocent who have no powerful relations are executed, the convicted criminals walk home as a free man after paying substantial amount of money.

CHAPTER TWO

How British Colonial Officers Taught Nigerians How To Steal

Professor Bayo Lawal, former Head of Department of History, University of Lagos and an expert in the field of History and Economics once went to China to attend the Confucius Institute's International conference. Confucius himself was a Chinese sage and philosopher who lived before Christ. The Chinese people who named the Institute after him are now poised towards spreading his philosophy and their cultural values, hence the invitation of Professor Lawal and other intellectuals around the world to study the Chinese culture. When he returned to Nigeria, we had discussions on the various issues including the problems of corruption and learning from history. He spoke on his various studies on corruption in Nigeria during colonial times. The interview is produced in this chapter to give more insight into the Chinese people, how the tackle corruption and how Nigeria found herself in the web of deceit. Excerpts:

Q: What is intriguing about learning History?

A: We need to know how the past led to the present. The past is a four – letter word. The past is very broad. It means many things. Are you talking of past ideas, past events, past values, activities, conflicts, wars; the causes of the wars and results of the wars. It could be past science, people's ingenuity and how they relate to the present. They could be economic activities families, kingship. You will have elements of continuity and change. Look at the natural environment. Don't we have sunrise and sunset? That's the work of God. What about the seasons? These affect our values when you have to be conscious of trends. Human experiences are global; Japan, America China etc have their own history as we do in Nigeria. You have to plan and be conscious of changing trends and use these so that we do not have problems. We have these Colonial problems here in Nigeria. But we have some ways of solving them by learning from others who were in the same position we are in today. We learn from their history and how they got over their problem. If you are talking about Japan, its industrialization. China – we have rejected China in this part of the world in terms of studies.

Q: You were in China for the conference on Confucius. Who was he?

A: Confucius was a Chinese Philosopher. I traveled by train to the Institute created in his name about 500 kilometres to the capital of the country. People came from Europe, America, Asia and Africa and we brainstormed on various issues. They were selling China to us. We were at Tiananmen Square. It's a huge place, its size about the size of the University of Lagos Campus.

Q: What were your impressions of the Tiananmen Square?

A: That was the place where many students were killed some years ago when there was a protest.

Q: What feelings did you get from the conference and what do you think Nigeria can benefit from China?

A: That has always been on my mind. From what I saw, I kept reflecting on what we can benefit and the level of development I saw made me to ponder when Nigeria will attain that level. All the streets of the Capital were sparkling. They have over 50 cities and I heard that the level of development is the same. Some people said the level of development in other areas is great and unequal. Anyway, they are well – organized. Even in their government offices, they are straight. Someone informed me that they attend to people fast and promptly as if there is a third eye watching them. Their streets are sparkling. Their elevators work efficiently.

Q: Let's talk about this feeling that it's like a third – eye watching. Last year, the head of their Drugs and Food Agency was executed for corruption. What do you think?

A: Corruption is not frequent in China at all. They jail people for corruption and if they find that the corrupt person merits execution, they do so. Even in Russia. It depends on the gravity of the offence. Come to think of Area Boys? There is no place for such nonsense there.

Q: Do they have the kind of transport system with the bus – conductors screaming there since they are also classified and developing nation? Because Nigeria is a place that this is common and we also say its developing nation?

A: No way. They have good buses. But it's not only in Nigeria that they scream for passengers. They have such a thing in Kenya. They have Matatu buses in Nairobi. I have seen Nigerian boys in Kenya doing odd jobs. They even sell second hand clothes on the streets of Nairobi. I have seen them. In South Africa, Nigerians are there doing all kinds of things. Although they do not have our kind of democracy in China, they are very straight forward and organized. Things work well there. Although everything is controlled from a central command – through their hierarchy. They allow women to play active roles. They are very sharp. The women are very brilliant and they are in key positions even in the army. Because of their Socialist Economy, they have moved forward. I have studied some things even in their energy sector and I know they have solutions to the energy crisis. The solutions to our problems are there. There is need for government to change its stand and mode of operation. They need to have a national ideology and pump money into it – to change people's mind set. We need to feed this into children from nursery to Universities. It has to go from top to the bottom. China has since changed and opened up since perestroika and glasnost era. If we set our goals in Nigeria, we can achieve it. The Chinese did this and financed several projects that transformed everywhere using discipline without diversion of fund. We don't have discipline leadership in Nigeria. Our leaders are not disciplined. We need a disciplinarian. We need someone who can curb some of our traditional rulers and their excesses too. If we are serious, the present government must rule by example. Not that those in government or ministers should be awarding contracts to themselves.

Q: Over the years, you have studied and researched into corruption in Nigeria. Your inaugural lecture was on that too. Why are you carrying out studies on corruption?

A: The title of my inaugural lecture is; Corruption in Nigeria – A Colonial Legacy. It's about how British Colonial Officers stole money in Nigeria through fraudulent methods – accounting fraud, braking open iron boxes of cash meant for staff Salaries. This was before the use of banks became fashionable in Nigeria I mentioned names of British Officers who were involved. Two panels were always set up. One panel was for whites and the other for blacks. There was a case in 1922 in Calabar. A white man decided they should be taking care of themselves before salaries came. And anyone in need could take from it. However, the secrets leaked and the black man was roped in while others were transferred out.

Q. Can you give us other examples?

A. Yes. There are other examples which I cited in my inaugural lecture.

The earliest report of embezzlement was made in 1901 involving one Mr. C. V. Lougland, an assistant accountant, who contravened the financial regulations and lost £88. Rather than accept the verdict of the board of enquiry which required that he refunded the money, he denied any knowledge of the requisite financial regulations and even attributed the loss to an unauthorized Nigerian clerk who had access to the box of money. The Secretary of State in reacting to the culprit's appeal for leniency ruled that the amount be written off. He was thereby saved from the hardship of making good the loss and the case was closed. The claim of ignorance of the requisite financial regulation was a pretext and a smart cover-up employed by Mr. Lougland. This cover-up was reinforced by his attribution of the loss to an unauthorized Nigerian clerk who was at large. The board of enquiry disbelieved his statement and thereby held him responsible although the Secretary of State ruled otherwise. In the same year, Captain Gonstedt, Master of 'Heron' at Lokoja, embezzled £3 out of government money. The loss was discovered while he was on leave in Britain. The Secretary of State ruled that whatever his defense and whether he returned to Nigeria or not, he should be dismissed forthwith. (Lawal, 1987).Losses of public fund by theft was again reported in 1902 at Ilorin, Kabba and Illo. The auditors held Major Hall of the West African Frontier Force responsible for the loss of £28 at Ilorin. On hearing about the charge, he deserted the army but was later apprehended by a search party for trial. After cross-examination, it was discovered that Major Hall did not comply with the Frontier Force Order 443 which reads "In cantonments and the line of March and on all occasions whenever possible, double sentries will invariably be posted on treasure". Rather, Hall placed the boxes of money under a guard, Private Awudu Zaria of 1st Northern Nigeria Regiment. According to an eye witness, Assistant Resident K. Dougan Harrison, the cash box was placed in the guardroom in his presence and was securely locked by Major Hall. He added that the key was still in Hall's possession until the robbery, which was alleged to have been committed about 4.00a.m. Wednesday 5 March, 1902, was reported to him by Sergeant Sharpe. It is interesting to note that the board of enquiry did not invite Private Awudu for interrogation and neither did it investigate the circumstances under which the loss was discovered. The board just considered the theft practicable because of lack of necessary precautions, the inadequate number of sentries, the portable nature of the dispatch box and the ease with which it could be hidden. In the end however, Major hall was exonerated and the amount was written of as irrecoverable. It is apparently clear that the board of enquiry intentionally begged the question of robbery and left important areas of the incident unexamined. For example, why was Private Awudu Zaria not interrogated? Why did Major Hall flee when he first heard about the charge? The board, while working in concert, did not bother to consider the possibility of making a duplicate key by the culprit. This is a classical procedure used by the colonial administrators to cover-up financial malpractices by their kith and kin. Another similar incident of theft of £250 at Illo was reported by the auditors in 1902 and Captain Maclachlan of Northern Nigerian Regiment was apprehended for embezzlement (Lawal, 1987). He protested against the decision of the board of enquiry, which demanded that he paid part of the loss. In his defense he stated that an empty cash box was mistakenly substituted for the locked one that contained money. While the empty one was kept in the guardroom, the one containing money was left outside and at night the box of money was stolen. It is ridiculous that on account of this single stupid behaviour, Lord Lugard got the consent of the Secretary of State to write off the loss. Thus far, the cases cited were symptomatic of perversion of administrative process in the colonial setting whereby European culprits were exonerated. The active involvement of the colonial governor and his administrative relationship with the colonial office already constituted a conversion network by which the captain was prevented from bearing the brunt of his negligence and carelessness. One can at this juncture notice the development of a trend in the perpetration of fraud by the colonial personnel whereby stories were concocted to escape the full penalty of their crimes. While fully aware of this rend, the various boards of enquiry tied to reverse it by applying rigid punitive measures. Perhaps this is exemplified by another case of theft of public fund by Mr. Kentish Rankin, Assistant Resident Kabba in 1902. While explaining to the board of enquiry how £28 was lost, he concocted a story that when he went to bed at night (because of his sickness), he kept the key to the safe under his pillow. While he was fast asleep, one of his servants abstracted the key from his bed and stole the money. Rankin could not produce any of his servants to testify; whereas it was discovered that he kept public money in his private quarters instead of complying with the financial instructions which demanded that he kept the money in the guardroom garrisoned by about forty soldiers. It was therefore clear that Rankin misappropriated the money and was thereby entitled to the full penalty of his crime, but Lord Lugard in his dispatch to the Colonial Office clandestinely attempted to reverse the verdict of the board of enquiry and demanded the Secretary of State to write off the loss on the ground that Rankin was ill when the money was stolen. The Secretary of State objected to his request and ruled that Rankin should refund the money. This was another case of outright violation of official instruction in order to embezzle public fund. The colonial governor repeatedly perverted the course of justice to safeguard the career of Rankin, contrary to the verdict of the board of enquiry. This was an example of aiding and abetting frauds by the godfathers of colonial officials. Similar fraudulent practices were also prevalent in Lagos Colony and Southern Nigeria among the ranks and files of some British personnel. In 1901, a British officer, Lieutenant Byrne, commanding the Detachment of Southern Nigerian Regiment at Ogota, lost £100 out of £600 being public money in his care for the payment of his men who were engaged in the Aro expedition. Byrne kept the money in the magazine, but at night the money was reportedly stolen. He was blamed for not keeping the money in the guardroom and was asked to refund £10 out of the total loss. The balance was written off as irrecoverable. Captain C. J. O'Connell of the West African Frontier Force was exonerated in 1904, from a charge of stealing £255 which was lost in transit from Degema to Owerri. According to the culprit, an anonymous deserter stole the money. Also in Lagos, a local auditor discovered in 1907 that Butler Wright, the Deputy General Manager of Government Railway, misappropriated £150 from the construction account. (Lawal, 1987). When called upon to account for the loss, he became nervous and dumb-founded. Neither could he concoct any story. He instantly paid back the money and no punishment was meted out to him. Indeed, between 1905 and 1906, the total sum recovered from culprits apprehended for fraudulent practices in Southern Nigeria was £942 while queries involving £640 were yet to be replied. Yet the central government did not relent in its effort to minimize these dishonest practices.

CHAPTER THREE

Introduction To Fraud And Scam

The Nigeria criminal code which frowned at Scams, Fraud ands crime of persuasion as it is called in some circles is Section 419. All crimes in this category are now generally known by members of the public and security officers as "419"

In colonial times when the post office was the only source of communication (carrying letters) from one place to the other 419, was known to have been done on very minimal levels. This was restricted to fast growing urban centres such as Lagos, Ibadan, Enugu and Kano mostly amongst literate family members who deceived their illiterate brothers and sisters. There were cases of government officials who deceived illiterate civil servants, or farmers in local areas etc. In those days, there were isolated cases of letters or messages being opened or decoded by officials or government workers. The information received was used for selfish financial gains. A retired civil servant once hinted how his cousin who was a sergeant in the Nigeria police opened a letter belonging to his uncle and spent the enclosed British pounds (meant to treat his ailment) in the 1950s. The man later died. In the post independence era, Nigerians heard about pockets of cases of deception, fraud, scams in government and private circles as noted earlier in the country's political history. Some cases were localized and centered on claim of doubling people money through fetish means. During the oil boom era, there were jobs for the people and the youths were gainfully employed. There were also very rare cases of telephone conversations either being tapped or letter being open by wrong hands. The socio-cultural and economic landscape of Nigeria changed dramatically and drastically to what we have today with fraudsters, con men and 419 people holding sway about 20years ago when the Ibrahim Babangida administration imposed IMF conditionally on the people through the devaluation of the currency overnight with a military decree. Critics argued that the regime also brought about what was known as the "settlement syndrome" whereby the leadership not only encouraged sealing political opponent's lips with cash, political appointments, but was also alleged to have engaged the deception and dribbling of the populace like the Argentine footballer, Diego Maradona. Some government insiders then claimed the government put in place those policies in the interest of the people. The populace gradually became lost in the political amnesia and the youths imbibed this new culture of deception to get what they wanted. Deception swept through the society like a hurricane into banks, religious places, marriages, schools, security agencies etc. Modernization of the communication systems, the telephone, fax machine, satellite television started and exposed the people to new information and technology faster than before.

Con artists and fraudsters allegedly began to tap people's telephones in connivance with insiders in some now moribund communication companies to defraud and rob visitors and indigenes returning from abroad. During this era, con artists, and criminals persuading people featured in the manner of "money-doubling" (otherwise known as "wash wash"). This entailed a fraudulent person claiming he has the capability to double people's money or converts the Naira currency to dollars or pounds sterling. Some of these criminals often claimed that they were either from Mars or other foreign planets, foreign countries, and could not speak English. They usually claimed they had ships berthing with goods (cement, milk etc at the wharf). They were noted to have power of hypnotism in some cases and going into people's homes and vanishing into thin air. Some even masqueraded as financial institution experts, from people looking for mega interest rates. Many of them disappeared to Europe and America.

SCAMS IN EUROPE AND AMERICA

The Western world has been known for over half of the millennium to have been structured along the line of deception, agreed and blood. Hundreds have left their countries, carried out invasion, conquered territories, deceived the people and took them as slaves. Then, there was colonization and neo-colonization and organised scams, both private and official which were exported to new overseas territories. The cash economy of the Western World completely changed the culture and values of the African society. The mechanism quest and desperation of the Western World swept through the Nigeria landscape too.

In modern times, it is not uncommon to see in the USA advertisements and notices which lure unsuspecting victims to scams in visa(s) (lottery) procurement, fake marriages, fake awards, fake job procuremen agencies, fake professions (work at homes), fake religious persons (and spiritualists), fake literary contests etc. The vast religious sanctuaries have become the "den of robbers" as Jesus Christ said in the Bible.

ELECTRONIC/INTERNET CRIME

In the United States and Europe, funds are being transferred electronically through banks and individuals. The advent of the internet in the 1990s has revolutionized the mode of financial transaction through the use of electronic/computers and the World Wide Web. There are banks that operate solely on the internet. Because of the new development, fraudsters, con artists and crooks are targeting electronic medium to deceive people and steal money.

The use of credit to purchase things at the market and settle all kinds of bills through the use of electronics has also become a feature of global transaction. However, fraudsters steal credit cards of others and use them to siphon money from people's account. In the same way, fraudulent people also steal other people's passwords to gain access into their accounts to withdraw their money. According to the Federal Bureau of Investigation (FBI) in the USA, 83 percent of funds are transferred through electronic means while 17 percent by cash. This means that unlike in Nigeria where people generally carry cash (or *Ghana must go bags*) to pay mostly through the pressing of a button on the computer, telephone or fax. Although the Western World is very advanced in the use of electronic to transfer money, there are instances of con artists and fraudsters stealing money electronically. In some of the few cases that exist, some bankers colluded to either defraud their customers electronically or outsiders steal their passwords to divert money. Some people describe the computer as garbage in, garbage out. When you feed fraud intent information into it, it will at the tail end indicate fraud, possibly after the originator may have stolen the money and bolted away.

NIGERIA AND GLOBAL DIMENSIONS INTO INTERNET CRIMES

Internet usage gradually entered the global information network in the early 1990s. By 1997, it crept slowly into the Nigerian society. Very few people were also aware of its usage. However, few organisations opened Cyber cafe centers at strategic locations and the few internet office boxes). You could have your passwords or have it securely kept by the owners of the cyber cafes. Two years later, cyber cafes began to spread into other parts of the city of Lagos. Ibadan etc. In the whole of Anthony village, Lagos there was one. In Surulere, the only cyber cafe was at the shopping complex. There was just one around the Obalende area. Then the scammers used fax and bugged telephone messages to defraud people. Between 1999 and the new millennium, internet usage boom had commenced, cyber cafes sprang like mushrooms everywhere. Unlike in the past where you paid to open e-mail addresses, yahoo, hotmail, Tec email and others offered e-mail services. Con artists shifted focus from telephone and fax to the internet. With the world becoming a global village through the internet, it was easier and faster for fraudsters in Nigeria to reach out to the nooks and crannies of the world. Their mode of operation and tactics changed drastically and desperately. Operators of 419 became more daring and dangerous. They seemed to have also been militarized by years of dictatorship and impunity which featured during the years of military rule which terminated on May 29, 1999.

Some of them were alleged to have operated in concert with some men in power and had even disguised (though secretly as workers) of the Central Bank of Nigeria, Nigeria National Petroleum Corporation, (NNPC), Minster(s) of finance, king(s), Chief(s) Prince(s). The CBN and NNPC have always dissociated their organizations from activities of these unrelenting and unrepentant fraudsters.

MODE OF OPERATION

No fewer than 3,000 names of prominent Nigerians have been used by scammers. Your name is likely to be on the list if you are; or have held key positions in government parastatals or industrial sector. Your organisation's names are likely to have been used to defraud, if you are into banking, oil, movie, mass communication, telecommunication or construction. The typical 419, operator(s) send(s) hundreds of letters blindly to innocent people all over the world.

They even claim to be religious men soliciting for assistance or victims of persecution who have millions of dollars that are waiting to be transferred to unsuspecting victims for a percentage or bogus projects they often claim to have constraints in transferring the funds to execute. They would seek your assistance to move the funds offering to give some percentages. Some have variously used the name of Mrs. Mariam Abacha who they are aware her husband stashed away billions of Nigerian dollars in various banks abroad to dupe unsuspecting foreigners. A school of thought argued that defrauding some of these foreigners was probably easy because they too were greedy. The language of the letters often used by fraudsters is usually full of spelling and grammatical errors. A newspaper editor in Kazakhstan once told me in Amsterdam how he received barrage of 419 letters from those who claimed to be Mrs. Abacha from Nigeria. Many oil companies including Shell, Chevron, and other multinational organisation's names have been used by tricksters. The advent of the GSM (the use of cell phones) has brought 419 home to very ignorant local people by tricksters who claimed they have won prizes from spurious lotteries and games.

The MTN Nigeria Ltd, Globacom Nigeria Ltd and Celtel now Zain and other GSM operators in Nigeria constantly sent disclaimers of such bogus claims. Fraudsters had even used the GSM to dupe innocent retirees and those who have relations abroad by claiming they have just returned from (their relations) overseas and they needed recharge cards to make calls before they can convert their foreign currencies to local ones.

Cyber crime has become a global concern in the new millennium. In Nigeria, many banks, institutions, and individual have been defrauded locally and internationally through the use of electronic medium of communication.

The Internet is the cheapest, fastest and out most abused media where people are susceptible to being defrauded by those who make bogus claims. The internet is one of the most abused media to impersonate.

There is need for an aggressive enlightenment campaign in Nigeria on the use and identification of con artist and their foreign collaborators.

CHAPTER FOUR

The Reign of Fraudsters

Cases of advance fee fraud popularly known as "419" in Nigeria have permeated religious centers, business organisations, academic, sports administration and other sectors of the economy

They called themselves "men of God". But recently they were docked at Igbosere Chief Magistrate Court over an alleged Advance Fee Fraud, popularly known as 419. The "men of God." are Godson Opara, Romanus Dike, Cletus Ajaero, Ifeanyi Onuaha Donatus Akalawu, Innocent Osuagwu and Udo Ojukwu.

The prosecution had alleged that the seven "men of God" at Embassy Guest Hall, Udo Hotel, Lagos attempted to obtain $12,000 from another man of God, Reverend Smith, from Houston, Texas, USA. They told Reverend Smith that the sum of N6.4 million would be transferred to the Nigerian government to permit the construction of an affiliate church in the country.

While the men were being tried for allegedly committing an offence punishable under Section 419 of the Nigerian Criminal Coder Cap. 31, Volume 11 Laws of Lagos State of Nigeria 1973, their fate was hanging over another offence: an alleged theft attempt.

The seven men, according to the prosecution attempted to steal the sum of N1.6 million from the same American, Reverend Smith at Owerri. The second offence is punishable under Section 509 of the Criminal Code.

Cases of advance fee fraud have become a source of concern. Criminals have found their ways into legitimate business organisations, academics, sports administration and other sectors of the economy.

Towards the end of last December, four members of an alleged "419 gang" were arraigned before the Miscellaneous Offences Tribunal (MOT). The four accused persons, Stanley Oduo, alias Dr. Duru Odika, Clifford Ovwarah, Charles Eze and Chuka IIomba were alleged to have conspired and obtained N2.6 million from a Danish national. The men who spent their Christmas and New Year in prison custody would be making frantic efforts to clear themselves when they appear before Justice Tijani Abdullahi in two weeks. It was alleged that the four men forged documents purported to have emanated from the Central Bank of Nigeria and the Nigeria National Petroleum Corporation (NNPC). These documents were said to have been faxed to someone for a non existent oil deal. It was claimed about U.S $10,000 was lost in the process.

The academic is not spared. A professor Greg who claimed that he is an expert in Chemistry prowled some parts of the Eastern states duping people. The fake professor told sympathisers he was stranded in Nigeria after his return from the USA. According to him, he had lost his wife and children through drowning and he needed money to quickly return to USA. In the process, he got money from several people. In Edo State, a man simply referred to as a "419 Chief" was nabbed for obtaining money under false pretence. The money which is about N127.8 million was taken from three unsuspecting victims.

Mr. Oyo Orok Oyo, second Vice-President of the Confederation of African Football (CAF) may not have recovered from the shock he suffered from the perpetrators of 419. Oyo's name was used for deception and his signature forged. The faceless con artists wrote to Turkish Soccer Federation. They even copied the Secretary General of the Union of European Football Associations (UEFA). Oyo was stupefied when he saw a copy of the letter faxed to Cairo's office of the Secretary-General of CAF. Mr. Moustapha quickly alerted members of UEFA, FIFA, NFA and WAFU. The authors of the fake letter would have succeeded in getting clearance to send their "officers as the nation's soccer administrators and ambassadors" to Turkey. The fake letter bored reference number CAF/UEFA/APP/VOL/01/96 and fax number 234-01-2662526.

Tom Chalmers, Editor of *World Air* news got a letter from one Oscar Ova. The said Ova claimed he lost his father who was a financial controller at the Nigerian Presidency in a ghastly motor accident. According to him, his late father had confided in him that he had $11 million in his penthouse. He wanted Chalmers to put down thousands of dollars to facilitate the transfer of the money. A smart Chalmers quickly saw the hands of 419 and he screamed aloud.

Some men who paraded themselves as Chiefs live off 419 scams. There was a case involving a prominent chief in Idemili local government, Anambra state. The chief was said to be a claimant to one of the thrones in the area. He had several of his exotic cars including Mercedes Benz class seized and packed at Alagbon, Ikoyi. Lagos. What was his offence? He was involved in 419 deal running into N23 million.

Acting on a petition from one Chief E.C. Anago Amanze who wrote on behalf of a British national, the authorities swooped on the chief said to have duped the British company, Ledrop Export Ltd, of 251, Rompton Road, London. When the Managing Director of the company visited Nigeria to recover his money, he was allegedly threatened. For fear of his life, he flew out and asked someone to act on his behalf.

Wherever Patrick Kilman, a Briton is today, he would think twice before paying any visit to Nigeria. Kilman who was on an errand was kidnapped and held in Onitsha by a suspected group of con artists before he was a rescued by the police.

Diplomatic sources in Lagos said that documents emanating from Nigeria are often treated with contempt abroad due to the nefarious activities of fraudsters and those who engage in advance fee fraud. These conmen are sophisticated and mobile. They are always on the move and hard to grab.

They can be found permeating all sectors of the economy. They falsified documents relating to services they do not offer.

Diplomats kept warning their nationals to ignore or disregard business requests from individuals in Nigeria. Two French detectives visited

Nigeria recently over a case involving a Nigerian businessman detained in France over NNPC documents found on him in Paris. The French Detectives came to find out if the documents were genuine.

The case of Adegboyega, a New York based Nigerian is stunning. Until his arrest and current travails, he ran a network of credit card fraud in New York. This clique defrauded Americans of thousands of dollars. He lived a robust lifestyle, dishing out gifts and cash. It is little wonder they called him, *"The King of New York!"* The King of Credit Card fraud made nonsense of America's advanced electronic banking system and siphoned thousands of dollars. He shuttled around the globe in style.

Once deported over his involvement in some shady deals. He acquired another passport and sneaked back to the United States. Rather than operate silently, the "king" was determined to let his colleagues in the crime world know of his return. He frisked through people's accounts. The U.S authorities were unaware of his return until he was caught in another criminal activity and his pasts unveiled. He is currently behind bars.

The perpetrators of 419 deals think their job is a simple one. In some parlance, they are called professional "Letter-Writers". They write letters to foreigners promising to let them have access to key people in the vital sectors of the economy who can move millions of dollars across the globe into their accounts. The unsuspecting foreigners it is argued are culpable because greed is the driving force. Nigerian "letter-writers, according to investigations now target countries in the Far East or Eastern Europe.

Sources said that their feeling is that western diplomats are governments have warned their citizens to be weary of letters coming from Nigeria. But in Eastern Europe where communism used to be way of life, information flow is rather slow. So, the target is aimed at the former communist block.

Security operatives are currently on the heels of a gang of fraudsters who invited a Croatian into Nigeria over a $20 million advanced fee fraud deal.

Robert Tomasevie, the Croatian arrived the Murtala Muhammed International Airport, Lagos with great expectations. Somewhere along the line, the dupes failed to impress Tomasevie at the airport. Two alleged members of the gang, one Moses Idowu and one Obi who claimed to be representing their director, Dr. Prince Joe who invited the Croatian was waiting to receive him somewhere. The Croatian was already suspicious.

He refused to follow them out of the airport. On realising the futility of their assignment, the two men forced their guest into one of the toilets in the arrival hall and made away with his DM 1,500 (about N78, 000) and other personal belongings. The case was later reported to the airport security. But Tomasevie was stranded. He had to contact his Belgian friend who lives in Lagos to facilitate his journey back home. How and why did Tomasevie come to Nigeria? Strangely, the Croatian disclosed he received the message about the deal with "Dr. Prince Joe". He gave Dr. Joe's number as 01-5890113 adding that he did not know how the gang got his name and contact address.

In a related development, a Korean Mr. Kim Lee was arraigned before an Abuja Chief Magistrate Court for allegedly taking part in "419"

Lee was accused of convincing with one Captain Mike Nzeribe now at large to deceive and defraud by claiming to have aviation oil to sell to some Nigerian businessmen.

The prosecuting police officer, Inspector John Udo told the court that the Federal Intelligence Bureau (FIIB) got information that the so-called Captain arrived at Abuja and lodged into Room 252, Agura Hotel waiting for Kim Lee.

With this information a police detective team led by Senior Superintendent of Police Musa Yerima went to the place and met Kim Lee in the room booked by Nzeribe. A search was conducted in the room and the team discovered fake U.S dollars.

A Bangladeshi parliamentarian, Syed Masud Reza considered himself very lucky. He would have fallen into the hands of conmen if officers of the Nigerian Immigration Service had given him entry visa.

The vigilant Immigration Officers found that Reza was on a $47.3 million (about N3.817 billion) scam mission to Nigeria. According to authorities, Reza was in Nigeria with forged documents and without a visa. He was invited by one Dr. Usman Beko now at large. In the letter of invitation titled "Permission to transfer $57 million in your account", Dr. Beko who claimed to be the General Manager Procurement and Management Service (PROMAS) a unit under the corporation indicated of the syndicated) have a part payment of $47.3 million in the Central Bank of Nigeria (CBN) awaiting remittance into foreign account of their choice.

The syndicate offered Reza 30 percent of the total sum should he comply with the request to provide the account and safe keeping of the fund until their arrival in Bangladesh. Ten percent was meant to balance each other expenses made both sides while the remaining 60 percent will be "for us the originators," the letter added.

In another development, a man and a woman were arrested at the Murtala Mohammed International Airport last July with a large consignment of suspected Advance Fee Fraud (419) letters intended for postage overseas.

The mail numbering about 50,000 post-marked with forged franking machine impressions were detected by airport security officials and men of the Nigerian Postal Services. They promptly alerted the Chairman of Task Force on Postal and Telecommunication Offences, Lt. Col. Olu Akinyode who ordered the arrest of the two and promised to investigate the case and arrest those behind the practice.

The evil of 419 cannot be better illustrated than the case of a London based businessman who hails from Oyo State. In order to claim the premiums of dead people in London, he journeyed to Ibadan where he exhumed a dead body and cremated it. The ashes were then taken to London to convince insurance experts so that he could claim the money belonging to the dead people. However, the situation turned sour when the insurance experts smelt a rat and alerted Scotland Yard. The INTERPOL stepped in. Despite the intimidation investigators, the culprit was arrested and he is currently cooling off behind bars in London.

Not too long ago, the American navy in Italy was infiltrated by Nigerian gang of heroin traffickers. The gang, flesh spots and Naples lure young people and American naval ratings with the carrots of "fat cash, all expenses paid weekend to Turkey". Worried Pentagon" officials were stunned that no fewer than 20 of their men had been recruited by Nigerian kings of 419 and drug. On a global scale, these men and women are tagged: the world's most proficient drug smugglers." On realising that military personnel are hardly checked- they went to recruit U.S naval personnel. They actually go for those carrying U.S passport and offer them between $25.000 to $30,000 for the dead. U.S naval officers had been investigating the smuggling of drugs over time under an operation code named "White Stallion". At the end of it all, they found Nigerians had infiltrated the ring and perhaps operating on what is known as the "Golden Crescent heroin trail" which rolls from opium plantations in Afghanistan, through refineries in Turkey and ending up in the heart of Europe and especially Italy."

ENVIRONMENTAL 419

The ring was uncovered by an officer who was on the trail of the traffickers. He was to be recruited by Nigerians who did not known he was actually on their trail.

The worrisome trend has even entered environmental protection. Not long ago, a dubious and faceless individual who called himself Godswill Olokun and claimed to be an engineer with the Ministry of Science and Technology in Nigeria approached some foreign companies requesting for Toxic Wastes to be shipped into Nigeria. At the time Olokun made tbe request, Nigeria had no such Ministry. What the country had was the National Agency for Science and Engineering Infrastructure (NASENI) with the office at Victoria Island, Lagos. Olokun who supposed to be an engineer in the ministry informed interested oversees arrangements which made it legal for its citizens to dispose wastes sought from foreign countries. Perhaps unknown to the so-called engineering, Nigeria is a signatory to the Basel Convention which forbids the Trans Boundary Movement of Wastes into Africa. In the dubious letter of request, Olokun however hinted interested persons to make the matter a top secret which should not be disclosed to anyone claiming that Ocean close to Calabar to dump toxic wastes. Olokun's request to make the matter a top secret was enough to convince anyone that the government may not have approved such deals.

It was this dubious method that was used by Mr. Gianfranco Raefelli, the Italian who dumped waste at Koko port in 1987. The Italian had informed Mr. Sunday Nana, the Nigerian that he was bringing materials to set up a pharmaceutical industry, but they turned out to be hazardous materials.

* * * *

Dubious claims by fraudulent immigrants believed to be of Nigerian extraction have now made the German authorities to tighten access to their social security fund. Sources said that some Nigerians were found to be involved in the racketeering. In a particular case, a Nigerian allegedly siphoning money from virtually every German State when in fact he was registered officially in one state. According to source, the Germans were stupefied and shocked beyond words. They subsequently began a process whereby such allowances are collected on the same day throughout the country.

A similar incident occurred in the United Kingdom where a young man who happened to be the son of a retired government military of funds allocated students. In a particular case he allegedly duped the local government of about 10,000 pounds. To carry out his nefarious activities the young man from a popular Nigerian family changed his father's named, falsified several documents to show that he had a very poor background. As a matter of fact, he changed their residential abode in the city of London. Curious local government officials detected irregularities in one of his claims and alerted the authorities.

The British press got wind of the story and sought the reactions of his father in their British mansion just as the boy was one of his BMW.

After threatening fire and brimstone, the news still filtered out with a photo of one of their castle-like mansion somewhere in Lagos.

Sources hinted that most Nigerians caught in the web of 419 are always given away by their high flying taste. The drive state-of-the-art cars and live in expensive mansions and Island.

Sources said that a young Nigerian girl cooling it off in a British jail would not have been caught if she had kept a low profile. It was gathered that she regularly flew out of London every weekend to various capitals around the world. This made security agents to be suspicious of her and her means of livelihood. They discovered she was riding Mercedes Benz and BMW series. On a closer look at her activities they found she had been burrowing into other people's accounts.

On of the lords of fraud now in detention in Lagos was known to be very generous at wedding ceremonies and other parties where he openly tore bundles of naira note and threw it up over the heads of recipients (newly weds). He does not stop the naira rain until it has formed a mountain of carpet beneath the feet of the couple. Today, he remains incommunicado in one of the prisons.

Recently in Owerri John Bosco Iwuala lost a substantial amount of money to some men suspected to be perpetrators of 419. The men collected to give him and promised to give him some textile materials known as *George* the scene under some strange excuses; Iwuala opened the contents of a big said to have contained the deposited textile materials and found them to have contained potatoes.

The spate of advance fee fraud cases was reported to have been one of the reasons why the Nigerian government banned the operators of business centres all over the country. It was believed that these centres were fax messages and other communication gadgets are used facilitated the sending of dubious and fraudulent messages. Nigeria's Telecommunications Minister, Major General Tajudeen Olanrewaju emphasized this throughout the duration of the ban while making alternative arrangements. It is equally believed in some quarters that 419 messages also go through mails. Mails are regularly torn open by dubious people who are believed to be acting on message and orders not sent to them.

Already, trade malpractice involvement a total of N1.5 billion was recorded by the Federal Government constituted Task Force received and treated 4482 petitions related to trade malpractice and money laundering throughout the country. According to the Chairman, Alhaji Mohammed Santuraki, the figure represents the total amount involved between January 1994, and January 1996. A breakdown of the treated petitions received in 1994, while a total figure of 2058 was received in 1995.

Only recently too, an employee a total the Nigerian Postal Service (NIPOST) and an hotel bar attendant were arrested in Ikeja areas of Lagos by men of the Task Force on Telecommunications and Postal Offences. They were alleged to have been in possession of 95 overseas postal packets. The arrested NIPOST staff was employed five years ago. He and his collaborators were known to have been diverting mails from abroad to this hotel. At the hotel, they opened the letter and dislodged the contents. T.A Shobanjo, the Public Relations Officer of the Task Force said the men will soon appear in court before the Special Tribunal on Miscellaneous Offences. In fact before the arrest of the NIPOST staff, Major General Olanrewaju warned that any property owner who allowed his premises to be used to violation of the Miscellaneous Office Decree "risk the forfeiture of such property to the government."

"What government is seeking with this decree is to put the onus on members of the public, particularly, landlords to be vigilant as to what their property are being used for, "he said.

CRIMINAL CODE LAW SECTION 419

Any person who by any false pretence, and with intent to defraud, obtains from any other person anything capable of being stolen, induces any other person to deliver to any person anything capable of being stolen, is guilty of a felony, and is liable to imprisonment for three years.

If the thing is of the value of one thousand naira or upwards, he is liable to imprisonment for seven years. It is immaterial that the thing is obtained or its delivery is induced through the medium of a contract induced by the false pretence.

The offender can not be arrested without warrant unless found committing the offence. 419 (1)

Any person who by any false pretence by means of any other fraud obtain credit for himself or any other person.

(a) In Incurring any debt or liability: or

(b) By means of any entry in a debtor and creditor account between the person giving, the person receiving credit, is guilty of felony and is liable to imprisonment for three years.

419 A (2)

The offender can not be arrested without warrant unless found committing the offence.

419B

Where in any proceedings for an offence under section 419 or 419A it's proved the accused-

(a) Obtained or induced the delivery of anything capable of being stolen, or

(b) Obtained credit for himself or any other person. by means of a cheque that when presented for payment within a reasonable or insufficient funds were standing to the credit of the drawer of the cheque in the bank on which the cheque was drawn, thing or its delivery shall be deemed to have been obtained by a false pretence accused issued the cheque he had reasonable grounds for be living and did in fact believe, that it would be honoured if presented for payment within a reasonable time after its issue by him.

* *This story was published in African Concord in 1997*

CHAPTER FIVE

Democracy, Fraud Schemes and Arrests

Professor Alex Gboyega, a political scientist wrote in the book; *Corruption and Democratization* in Nigeria published in 1996 by the German organization, Fredrich Ebert foundation, Lagos about his experiences under the military regime. Gboyega noted under the title *Corruption and Democratization in Nigeria, 1983-1993. An overview,* the terrible state of corruption under the military from the Buhari regime to Babangida's government. However, the Professor appeared not to have envisaged the horrible level of greed and corruption which the Nigeria democrats later brought to power under the regime of ex-President Olusegun Obasanjo. But we should add too that Obasanjo himself was a former military leader even though he later wore civilian garment under democracy. It should be pointed out that during the General Ibrahim Babangida regime, one of the most vociferous critics of Babangida was General Olusegun (rtd). Obasanjo even lambasted Babangida of establishing a culture, called "Settlement". This phenomenon entails bribing or inducing, critics and cronies alike to do the President's bidding. This was also part of the legacy of Obasanjo's civilian government. The regime produced many more corrupt persons and idle minds who took to ploys to defraud. He also created the EFCC which fished out such corrupt individuals in and outside government. Some of them were tried and convicted as you will read subsequently. After Babangida toppled the Buhari/Idiagbon military government, Alex Gboyega recalled that the Political Bureau set up by that regime cited examples of how corruption permeated the Nigeria society through officials who took advantage of their offices to acquire wealth or other personal benefits. What is Corruption? Some Nigerian officials hardly realise that corruption "Involves giving or taking bribe or as in the words of Professor Gboyega, "acquisition of wealth using the resources of a public office, including the exercise of discretion.

"Incidents of illegal acquisition of wealth reached unprecedented levels during the Babangida administration "says the Professor adding that the former military President promoted so much corruption during his regime because he wanted people to be more loyal or amenable to his political manoeuvres. Governance in Nigeria is complex and unpredictable. Perhaps if Professor Gboyega realized that the Olusegun Obasanjo would later come to power few years after and preside over a grandiose pseudo civilian/military democracy, it is doubtful if he would have quoted Obasanjo for lambasting Babangida's government for " choosing a moment when they (people) are most vulnerable to step in with generous assistance, to fly them or their dependants abroad for life saving medical treatment, or favours of lifting oil or supplying fertilizer – patrimonial governance. M.O. Maduagwu in his treatise on Nigeria in search of Political Culture: The political class, corruption and Democratization hints that corruption thrives in Nigeria because the society sanctions it. He had recalled in 1996 that no Nigerian official would be ashamed, let alone condemned by his people, because he or she is accused of being corrupt adding that the corrupt official will be hailed as being smart.

"Any government official or politician who is in a position to enrich himself corruptly but failed to do so will, in fact, be ostracised by his people upon leaving office. He would be regarded as a fool, or selfish or both," says Maduagwu

A school of thought noted that what Obasanjo accused Babangida of doing was committed by the same Obasanjo to stay in power and used to try to extend his stay in power for another term. There were several cases of those prosecuted and convicted by the EFCC during the new civilian rule. For example, the Economic and Financial Crimes Commission (EFCC) in 2007 arraigned a 28-year-old man, over economic crimes. Others were arraigned in absentia. They are: Enyinnaya Nwokeafor and Nnamdi Chizoba a.k.a Yellow Man, Abdul Rahman, Michael Aderson, Edmund Walter, Nancy White, Anthony Friday Ehis a.k.a John J. Smith and Kesandu a.k.a Keke. The prosecution said that the accused and others had between 2002 and 2006 obtained money running into millions of dollars from people in the United States indigenes under false pretences. It was noted that Nwokeafor, in one of his antics claimed he was one Eric Williams, a very rich old man suffering from throat cancer, who needed a trustworthy agent to help dispense $55 million dollars charity fund to the underprivileged in the US from his base in Amsterdam because of his inability to travel to USA.

The fraudster was said to have asked for money to clear some of the expenses and he reportedly got $38,000 through Western Union Money Transfer in Amsterdam.

The notorious con artist was said to be on the wanted list of security agencies all over the world for duping people across the globe. He was said to have dropped out of University of Benin in 1998 and traveled Amsterdam but was once deported over immigration problem. In another case, Justice Tijani Abubakar of the Federal High Court in Lagos, convicted one 24 years old undergraduate, Mr. Silas Stephen Uwem for operating a bank account with the Access Bank Plc which was believed was used for money laundering of illegal funds. Apart of convicting the university student, Justice Abubakar ordered that the N16m, found in the bank account of the convict, should be forfeited to the Federal Government of Nigeria. It was also the EFCC, the Economic and Financial Crime Commission that prosecuted the case against the student who was an undergraduate of the Lagos State University, Ojo. The student was said to have a total of N16m in his Access Bank account and it was believed that he obtained the money through Internet scam. It was claimed that the undergraduate carried out some of his scam activities through chatting with people on the internet. During the case, the student alleged that that his father also gave him part of the N16m. But this was refuted by his father, who said what he gave his son was just N250, 000.

The judge later warned the convict to be a better person after serving his prison term.

Thomas Katona, 56, a one time treasurer for Michigan's Alcona County was arrested and charged in the United States for allegedly embezzling $1.2 million in public funds some of which were said to have been sent to Nigerian con artists or 419 persons who lured him with an email.

Katona was arraigned in the district court on 10 counts, including embezzlement and forgery.

The prosecution's Attorney General Mike Cox said that Katona directed eight unauthorized transfers of his county's monies. The transfer was said to have been done when he was on a visit to London in 2006. According to the prosecution, six of the transfers were made to banks in Nigeria known to have connections some fraudsters.

According to reports of the investigation, Katona also wired $72,500 from his own account despite the fact that he was warned by bank officials that they suspected he could have been sending money to con artists in Nigeria.

This was the end of a glorious career for Katona, who had served as county treasurer from 1993 until he was dismissal in November, 2007.

Three Nigerians, Jolly Akpoge, Michael Ogbile and Cyrus Ovie, were arrested in December 2007 at the Murtala Muhammed International Airport, Ikeja, Lagos for allegedly conning a Chinese lady the tune of about 3,000 Euros, The men were nabbed when they went to receive the Chinese woman known as Tseung C. Barbara when she arrived Nigeria aboard China Southern Airline. The lady was allegedly deceived by the men that she was to meet her French male friend who had a rift with her. However, she was stunned when she arrived Nigeria to meet black faces at the airport instead of her French friend. The stunned lady created a scene which attracted security men who found out what had happened and subsequently arrested the con artists and detained them at the airport police station. A member of the gang, according to reports had pretended on the internet as if he was the French male friend of the Chinese seeking reconciliation of their differences. There were indications that the identity of the Chinese lady and her relationship with the French man may have been revealed by a Nigerian who once lived in China.

There are some rich Nigerians whose names have been associated with deception. As the adage goes, the source of some people's wealth can be filthy. In December of 2007, a Nigerian socialite based in Lagos popularly known as Ade Bendel (whose real name is Mr. Ade Alumile) was sentenced to six years imprisonment for duping an Egyptian General of the sum of $600,000 in 2003.

The sentence was passed by an Ikeja High Court presided by Justice Muniru Olokoba. The EFCC handled the case which indicated that Ade Bendel claimed to be the owner of a company called Worldwide. He was said to have approached the Egyptian General with one Olafemi Ayeni in 2003 to cajole the General to release the sum of $600,000.00 which they said would enable them "buy chemicals that could be used to clean some paper notes". According to the prosecutors, the company never existed and the whole deal was a scam. The Egyptian had complained to the EFCC and this led to the arrest of Ade Bendel and his prosecution. The judge also ordered that the $600,000 should be recovered and paid to the General.

Despite the pleas of his counsel to Ade Bendel that the judge should temper justice with mercy, Justice, Muniru Olokoba said "the offence is an international embarrassment to the nation and the court does not have mercy with such offence" adding that to serve as deterrent to the present generation and the upcoming generation not giving the accused a full weight of the law is inappropriate.

A thirty nine years old Nigerian known as Henry Oshingbene, who lives outside the country was charged for allegedly duping people to the tune of $5,000. His style, according to the prosecution was to contact residents in the U.S. with a bogey information that they had won one million euros in a lottery. Oshingbene, it was alleged told his victims that they however needed to pay fees to get the money. Two victims were said to have lost more than $290,000. There are indications that the con artists have penetrated countries in Europe, North and South America duping people who fell for their schemes.

Con artists use several schemes and ploys to dupe people just like the story which I did below for the Sunday Vanguard illustrates.

American organizations and concerned individuals last week unveiled a new type of crimes of persuasion, known locally as 419 carried out by Nigerian con men through the use of dogs and their puppies. In this new wave of 419, Nigerian fraudsters are said to be luring prospective and unsuspecting buyers of dogs and lovers of puppies to buy these domestic animals that are non-existing through the internet. Last year alone the concerned groups, including the Council of Better Business Bureaus, the Humane Society of the United States, the Internet Crime Complaint Centre and the American Kennel Club disclosed that about 700 Americans were defrauded through the sale of puppies on the internet.

For each fraud, the con men reportedly stole between N40, 000 and N300, 000 through the sale of imaginary puppies. According to reports, though some of the fraud may have originated from within the United States, but Nigerian con men were particularly fingered in the ones that originated from overseas. In these schemes to make money from unsuspecting pet lovers, con men are said to have created websites indicating that they have puppies for sale.

They use two types of tricks which involve what is being described as overpayment scam in which a fraudster contacts someone and negotiates a price and later sends payment for the animal in form of a cashier's cheque. However, the fraudster would ask the potential victim to return the overpayment through an electronic transfer, back to the fraudster or a third party.

The report by Leslie McFadden added that "the victim eventually learns the cashier's cheque is counterfeit and loses the money he or she was supposed to get for the dog, plus any funds wired to the scammer. If the victim actually sent the dog, he or she won't get it back.

In the case of Nigerian 419 men using pets, the Americans warned on the internet last week that the con artists run advertisements on web sites they specifically created for the ploys and offer purebred puppies - typically English bulldogs or Yorkshire terriers - either free or at a discounted price.

The con artist then claims the animal is free or discounted. They also lie further that the owner is a missionary who has been looking for a new home for the dogs who has been suffering from terrible weather or climatic conditions in her present location or that the dog needed a new home after she was rescued from terrible natural disaster

Unsuspecting victims would then be asked to pay for the shipment or transportation of the dog, payment for inoculation and other fees. When the victims pay for all these, the dogs are never sent and the con men keep asking for more money and they give reasons for the delay in transportation.

Nigerian youths and students are getting caught in the web of 419 both locally and internationally. For example, a 25-year-old undergraduate, Mr. Omoniyi Sanlola, was on sentenced in 2007 to 34 years imprisonment by a Federal High Court in Lagos. He was sentenced by Justice Tijani Abubakar for engaging in fraudulent activities and forgery. It was the EFCC who prosecuted the case against the student on a 34-count charge of fraudulently and knowingly forging United States Postal Services money order payable to various people the previous year. It was such a pity that Sanlola, a final year student of Geology at the Ogun State University, Ago-Iwoye, ended up in the web of scam. The student had earlier had pleaded guilty to the 34-count charge preferred against him. However, it was the operatives of the National Drug Law Enforcement Agency stationed at the Ogun State border that arrested the student while on his way to the Republic of Benin. The Drug Agency officers found on the student seven sealed envelopes containing 34 forged postal order cheques. The student was expected to spend one year in jail because his term was to run concurrently.

Some con artists are not even afraid to use the name or sanctuary of God to dupe people. A fake pastor was picked by the police after they trailed him following complaints by the Redeemed Christian Church of God in Gbagada area of Lagos that someone was using the name of the church to dupe a foreigner. The suspected fake pastor, named as Isong, was picked for allegedly duping a foreigner of N3.5 million, using the name of Redeemed Christian Church of God (RCCG). Isong allegedly operated as Pastor Patrick Mark One

Nigerian named Babatope was caught in the web of scam baiters who are determined to divert the attention of those who are fully involved in the 419 industry all over the world.

The scam baiters are those who are determined to waste time and money of con artists who want to swindle people.

Babatope was caught in the web of a fictitious Church of A typical 419 scam e-mail will seek your help in liberating a sum of money, often tens of millions of dollars, in which you will share once the deal is complete. After the scammer establishes a relationship with you, he or she then requests money, often to offset "transfer fees," bribe officials, or otherwise eliminate some snag that stands between you and a million-dollar pay day. The scam baiters have created sites such as scamorama.com, 419eater.com, scambusters.org, thescambaiter.com, and a host of others where they parade con artists who have been caught in their tricks.

CHAPTER SIX

Cyber Crime 419 and the Nigerian Oil Industry

Two well dressed young men drove into the premises of an organisation sometime ago. They wore gold chains around their necks and wrists as they emerged from a sparkling with Mercedes Benz car. This was a symbol of affluence in Lagos. These men had approached a friend about their supposed contacts with top officials of the Nigerian National Petroleum Corporation (NNPC) and ability to influence the sale or movement of crude oil outside Nigeria. My friend who was interested in getting into the oil industry and the meeting to guide him and at the same time asset him in whatever capacity deemed fit. We greeted the two young men as they entered the office. We soon got into discussion and we went through the documents they brought to convince my friend about the business of lifting crude oil. As we went through the papers, I was stunned but dared not raise my doubts instantly for fear of reprisals. The documents were far from being genuine. They were fake. They were full of grammatical errors, inaccuracies; spelling errors and wrong address. You begin to wonder how a whole oil giant like the Nigerian NNPC could have allowed such badly written and disjoined letter(s) making uncoordinated and bogus claims said to have originated from the organisation. The letter which was said to have originated from NNPC was printed from someone's address on the internet. I gave some encouraging words to the duo that could not even speak a correct sentence in English, but discouraged my friend as soon as the men left. My friend told me afterwards that he informed the guys he was not interested in the business. Con artists and those involved in what is known seem to have invaded the oil industry in the country within the last few years with ferocious intensity. They claimed to have various papers, contacts and approval to lift oil from Nigeria. They used the names of the key oil players such as; Shell Petroleum Development Corporation, Chevron Nigeria Ltd, Exxon Mobil etc apart from NNPC and Department of Petroleum Resource (DPR). With the growing use of the internet, its availability, speed and affordability, fraudsters are reaching all the nooks and crannies of the world with bogus non existing deals and using the names of genuine oil companies and organisation in vain, Officials of the NNPC are alarmed and concerned about the effect of fraudulent deals on genuine investors. Apart from luring their victims to invest their money in the oil business; they often sent invitation letters to them to lure them into the country. Some victims of 419 letters into Nigeria have lost either their lives or possession. The United State Secret Service constantly sent warnings to American Embassy and her citizens asking them to ignore any letter emanating from persons in Nigeria who assure them that they can visit Nigeria without a visa. Some American institutions have requested their campus communities to report any letter soliciting for money or claming to have capabilities to export crude oil to the authorities. It is not yet known how much the oil industry in Nigeria is losing daily or monthly to fraud in the industry. It was found however that Shell Petroleum Company is concerned and has also issued warnings against Con artists to protect her corporate image and financial growth. Some fraudsters also shifted from the use of internet to the G.S.M. Cell phone. They prizes to some people over a game (or lottery) they did not play! Chevron too is alarmed about the use of her name by fraudsters who have become very elusive in their schemes. The Economic and Financial Crimes Commission too had issued guidelines to operators of cyber cafe in Nigeria.

TIPS ON HOW TO AVOID BEING DEFRAUDED ON THE INTERNET

1. Do not reply unsolicited mails from unknown people.

2. Do not call or reply anyone who claims you have won prizes or lotteries you did not play.

3. Sign out properly after using the Internet.

4. Do not expose your passwords.

5. Avoid exposing your relation's addresses overseas.

6. Do not be careless with your ATM cards, passwords or give out your account number to individuals you did not carry out legitimate business with.

7. If you live abroad and you have to carry out any project at home, use some private investigators, other parties to verify certain claims and information you are being supplied, even by relations.

8. You have to be very careful about any online business where a party says that you should not share the information about the initial transaction with anyone.

CHAPTER SEVEN

419 Relationships and Marriage

It sound rather strange and amazing that something like "419 relationships or phenomenon exists. But it is real and it is global. The process is gradual, deceptive, dangerous and Satanic like the traditional scam and fraud. This type of relationship has its apron string tied around the global prostitution racket. I have personally encountered and even had cause to save some Nigerian girls who would have found their ways into multimillion dollar prostitution industry in Italy or wasted away in Nigeria.

THE FIRST STORY: In the mid 1990s, a man walked up to one of my friend's offices to announce that this sister has been offered a job in Italy and that the employers were going to provide her with a free ticket, pay for her passport, visa etc. Immediately, I smelt a rat when I got to know that someone who secured the plum Italian job was also organising the whole trip. Their family had even begun to celebrate. I told this guy to be cautions and to ask the man giving the offer to produce official documents relating to the Italian job and the anticipated trip. Few days later, the girl's brother informed me that the man who was making the offer could not substantiate it when he was being questioned and that he had vanished.

SECOND STORY

Visa Lottery Scam: A man in his thirties walked up to a working class woman, and told her he has put her name on the America Visa Lottery Programme because he wanted to get her and her family out of the poverty circle.

The woman who was already engaged to another man and was about to get married was so excited and thankful. Few months later, the man returned to inform her that both of them had won the visa lottery and are expected to travel to America as a married couple because he filled the form claiming she was his wife. "No problem," retorted the lady who promptly discharged her husband and took this con artist to her parents and introduced him as her new man, who will be taking her to America. Everyone was happy in the family and they all began to celebrate.

I head about the development and had cause to send congratulatory message to the lady, But unknown to us, this con artist who claimed to be a scientist from a leading Nigeria University had be claiming money on a regular basis from this lady and assuring her that the processing was almost through from his brother who resided in New York.

This fellow took the woman to the passport office where they posed as husband and wife. For everything he supposedly did to facilitate the "Travel", he took money from the woman who had as good job by the Nigerian standard.

One day, a curious relation approached me with the documents with which the con artist was using to cajole the woman. He wanted to know if it was authentic. I looked at the Papers. They bore address in New York with the city's telephone code and numbers. There were, however grammatical errors, disjointed and uncoordinated type phase and no reference to the American Embassy in Lagos. I then asked the woman's relation to inform the man to take them to the consular section of the US Embassy in Lagos. They doubted my stand because this fellow used to phone someone who he claimed was his brother in New York through those phone numbers on the paper and everything appeared real.

Whenever he received foreign calls, foreign phone numbers would appear on his cell phone. Therefore, no one doubted him until he was asked to take them to the consular officer's office at the US Embassy in Lagos. Then the man began to shiver. He later confessed. He had siphoned money from the woman, disrupted her marriage, and shattered her American dream. She however still had her job and had not resigned.

THIRD STORY

I was in a place somewhere in Oshodi, Lagos when a woman came to make a call to someone in the United Kingdom. Their conversation was as follows:

Lady   It is me, Lynda calling you
                to wish you a happy birthday

Man: Lynda, how are you?
                Thank you for the call.

Lady: I am fine. I am currently in Amsterdam
                And I will soon be going to France for the
                Business I told you.

I was stupefied, wondering if the back of the building where I was located at Oshodi, Lagos that day was indeed Amsterdam. The woman began to talk of her love for the man and so on and I almost shouted; it is a lie! From the room as I overheard her conversation with the person in U.K, I began to wonder in my mind; is this person truly in UK too. Phone sim cards from United Kingdom are sold in some parts of Lagos. Besides, someone could roam his phone and the original number in any part of the country would appear.

This development is not peculiar to Nigerians. The advanced level of technology aggravated deception which has not been known in traditional Nigerian society, marriages and relationships. Nigerians, following the slave trade era have exported their kit and kin who were either forced into the plantations or house of their master as wives in the Americas.

419 LETTERS AND CONVERSATION

Thanks for your e-mail but one thing I must let you know is that no matter what, you can never be as smart as I am.

I know you are a Nigerian trying to fool yourself. I know much about this game, so if you are trying to dupe me, you are the same person that is acting for the Hotel. Bloody bastard, 419 operator. Bye for now hole," writes an American lady being lured by a Nigeria 419 operator.

After reading the above letter, the Nigerian 419 operator writes angrily back to the American:

"Hello Mugu,

Thanks for your (sic) letter but I want to let you to know one thing, you had better stayed away from computer else you will (sic) keep on paying unnecessary money away. Look at you lunatic, fool, bloody hill like you. See you internet mugu. F...k you like murder (sic) fu.ker look you. It is better for you to remove your name on the internet or else I will dupe you in another style which you will not expect.

Thanks, wise mugu like you."

Mugu is a derogatory Nigerian word used to describe one who is gullible.

419 NETWORKS IN SOUTH AFRICA

The internet conversation between the Nigerian 419 operator and the American lady clearly illustrates the type of dubious business practiced by Nigeria scam operator. From time immemorial, scam appears to be one of the oldest professions. It is based on bogus claims. But how do we describe the modern day 419 which began in Nigeria about 15 year ago? The scenario of the modern 419 which started in modern times involves someone faxing a letter to someone he barely knows. The scam has spread to other parts of Nigeria. Worse it has reached other West African countries and even South Africa where a Nigerian syndicate set up what was described as an "elaborate fake South African Reserve Bank website". Nigeria's 419 has reached a dangerous dimension with the global use of internet Nigeria Spammers use different cyber cafes to send messages across the globe seeking financial assistance with false claim of having millions of dollars stashed away in their care but unwilling to use the money due to either years of dictatorship or official bureaucracy. It was discovered that these con artists always claimed to be relations or former African heads of State like, Laurent Kabila, Mobutu Sese Seko, Sani Abacha and even the late Nigeria Attorney General, Chief Bola Ige. The Nigerian syndicate in South African Reserve Bank website scam had promised victim millions in return "for their assistance in moving vast amounts of money out of African countries."

South African detectives arrested 15 suspects during raids in Johannesburg area of Randbury and Sandston where the Nigerians lived. Most of the victims of the syndicate were Britons Americans. In an elaborate network, the syndicates also setup a website for a fake law firm that claimed that the illegal Reserve Bank was the authentic one.

Today, scams have permeated virtually all known and revered professions such as: law, medicine and religion. Some Nigerians living abroad often received calls from some Nigerians who posed as medical doctors claiming that their parents were on admission in the hospital and that the family would need some money urgently. These people were urged on to use the Western Union to transfer the money.

In a particular case a lady was saved from being duped when her friend, a nurse who coincidentally was on a visit asked the con artists to describe the nature of the illness but they could not describe it. In the South Africa Reserve Bank story, the South African Police was able to pick up the Nigerians after a tip off on their fake website.

Ironically, on the day that Milam Nuhu Ribadu the Chairman of Economic and Financial Crimes Commission was parading suspects of alleged 419 operators on television, this writer was a cyber cafe to use the internet, so were some suspected Con artists in the cyber cafe who looked away from television and continued to send their scam letters.

A victim of South African syndicate said he lost 2 million Rands after being lured through the fake website. South African Police said they were able to trace more of the syndicate's victims. The police indicated rather amazingly that the fake law firm which backed the crooks carried photographs of all alleged attorneys as well as a cell phone numbers which the police "established were diverted telephone lines in Nigeria and the United States."

South Africa police spokesman said, "The syndicate was extremely well organised. The main people are sitting in Nigeria but they have their runners here. There is a guy in Nigeria pretending to be Williams Sithole who has a law firm in South Africa." He noted that, the police big catch in the investigation came when a syndicate member diverted a cell phone for a single day and "from one lead we picked up a Sandston address and we found a lot of 419 letters there."

It was gathered that the syndicate's "victims were often asked to pay into an account in Taiwan and Monaco held by legitimate companies that exported goods to Nigeria."

The South Africans found "there is someone in this syndicate right at the top who had been importing goods to Nigeria from all over the world and the victims of the scam are paying for the goods." Nigeria's image in South Africa has been worsened by activities of Spam. In fact, an office has been set up to specifically fight 419 cases from Nigeria. In a joint operation with Scotland Yard, the South Africans arrested two people believed to be the originators of 419 letters in Roodeport, South African. When investigations took the police to a rented house in Rivonia, they found over 200 envelope with 419 letters addressed to businessmen and women all over the world!

So, far it is believed that some Americans who were lured into Nigeria with 419 were killed in the process of attempts to squeeze dollars from them by syndicate. The United States Secret Service is worried and sick about this development. They have also set up office on 419 cases in their embassy to specifically tackle scam letters and issues emerging from Nigeria. The U.S Secret Service has set up a website to advice its citizens on 419 mode of operation. The website says potential recipients of letters should be wary of letters from a Nigerian claiming to have been involved in over invoiced contracts or that he is an official of the Nigerian National Petroleum Corporation (NNPC) desiring to transfer money ranging from $10 recipient will have a share of 30 percent of the funds.

The United States Secret Service states that while sometime ago an American was killed in Lagos; other foreign nationals have been reported missing also.

The U.S secret service according to reports, receives about 100 telephone calls from 419 victims and 300-500 pieces of related correspondences per day.

Worse, some American universities and offices have also set up hotline numbers and have informed their staffs and student to refer any letter from Nigeria soliciting money. Unknown to some of the 419 letter writers, Nigerians also work in some foreign institutions where they wrote letters claiming to be either Mrs. Maryam Abacha, or Mrs. Imelda Marcos of Philippines.

THE DEADLY N23 BILLION 419 DEAL

The 419 problem is growing into a monster. In 2003, the U.S deported 76 Nigerians for alleged involvement in 419 and drug trafficking. Dr. Bolaji Aluko, a Nigerian based in US, said; "419" schemes originating from and inside our country are becoming a matter of life and death nothing that soon, our relations at home who genuinely have a medical condition will suffer from our attempts to verify all over the place whether their condition is indeed genuine, just in order to prevent our being "scammed".

As for me, I intend to pay Western Union to take a picture and finger print of whoever comes to claim money that i send to Nigeria. I am prepared to pay two percent on service charge for that!"

Dr. Aluko added; some of the other 419 schemes are just unbelievably cruel. I am aware that there are many Nigerians who believe that the traditional "419" where a crook meets a potential (usually white and western) crook serves that potential birth to a new monster in a humanly deadly manner and we are all losers for it."

****

A 72 years old retired Czech who was said have been swindled in a 419 deal by some Nigerians appeared to have vent his anger on Mr. Micheal Waydi, a 50 years old Nigerian diplomat gunned down inside the Nigerian Embassy in Prague.

The angry Czech also wounded a 31 years old clerk working in the embassy before surrendering himself to the embassy's guard force.

Those who are sending 419 letters out of Nigeria may think they are having fun or doing business, but they have callously damaged the country. In fact, Nobel Laureate, Wole Soyinka said in media reports that operators of 419 letters are chasing genuine investors away from Nigeria.

What Nigeria letter writers did to a Brazilian businessman, Nelson Skaguchi who was a director of Banco Noereste Brazil was terrible. The letter writer swindled the man 32 billion Naira which is about the budget of Lagos state which inhabits more than 7 million people!

It began in 1994 when in Enugu businessman introduced the Brazilian to some individuals who posed as controllers of the Central Bank of Nigeria. One of them even claimed he was Chief Paul Ogwuma, the former Central Bank's Governor while another claimed he was his deputy governor. The Brazilian had come to Nigeria to explore business opportunities before he fell into the hands of con artists. By the time he realised what was going on, he had lost $18.6 million (N23 billion). He lost his job as the director of the Brazilian Bank and was declared wanted by the police when auditors discovered he had mopped up all the money from the Brazilian Bank and his father in laws' company. The Nigerian letter writers were said to have one of those who swindled the Brazilian ended up buying one of the largest shares in one of Nigeria' foremost banks and became a director until he was discovered and removed. For the Brazilian, he became a fugitive. He ran away from his country and was believed to be living in fear some where he heard that one of those who met him to commence the swindle died mysteriously afterwards.

The Nigerian 419 deals have even put a dent on religious practice. One Mr. Hardarson who was sharing his experiences in the hands of 419 letter writers said; "they claimed to be Christians, quoted various verses of the scripture, lied they had prayed and fasted before calling me in hopes that they would be allowed to help me get the payment an thus benefit from it also. What make me really said it not the $6 to 7,000 I sent them which I can overlook but grieve that people would involve the most precious possession of their faith in a scam!

SAMPLE OF 419 LETTERS

From "DR. MRS. MARIAN ABACHA mm579mm@yahoo.com

Date: Fri 17 May 2002 10:59:53+0100

Reply to: "DR. MRS MARIAM ABACHA" mm579mm@yahoo.com

Dear Sir,

I am DR. MRS. MARIAM ABACHA, wife of the late Nigeria Head of State, General Sanni Abacha who died on the 8th of June 1998 while still on active duty. I am contacting you in view of the fact that we will be of great assistance to each other likeness (sic) developing a cordial relationship. I currently have the sum of Twenty four Million US Dollar (US$24,000,000.00) cash in a vault of a certain security company which I intend to use for investment, like Real Estate Development specifically in your country. This money came as a payback for the failed debt buy back contract deal between my late husband and some foreigners. I must inform you that the foreigners tried what they felt were good for the deal they had with my Late Husband and at the end of the present government says it was scam on our countries multi-billion debt to IMF, World Bank and Paris Clubs.

The Partners returned my husband's share of US$24,000,000.00 after the death of my husband and lodge (sic) in my husband's security company of which I am director until now, the new Civilian Government have intensified their probe on my husband's finances and Business Empire. In view these, I acted fast to withdraw the US$24,000,000.00 from the company's vault and deposited it in another West African Security company in Accra-Ghana. No record ever existed concerning the money traceable by the government because there is no documentation showing that we received the money from the foreign partners who did the business with Abacha and the fund was paid cash, so it has no traces from the bank.

Due to the current situation in the country concerning government attitude towards my family, it has become quite impossible for me to make use of the money within. Let me refer you to the front page of *Thisday* newspaper of 10th March 2001. you can log on to this various websites and get more details about my family, funds being recovered and how we are being subjected to different treatments to (sic) the name of searching for looted funds of my late husband.

www.thisdayonline.com/archieves/2001
http://www.guardian.co.uk/business/story/0.36043.563533.00.html and Newsweek international magazine of March 13-15th 2000.

The present government in Nigeria had frozen and seized all my work accounts both there in Nigeria and abroad. Thus on your consent to proceed in the business I shall expect you to contact m urgently to enable us discuss in detail about this transaction. Bearing in mind that your assistance is needed to transfer this fund, I proposed 20% of the total sum to you for the expected service and assistance, 10% offsetting expenses incurred the course of this transaction.

Your urgent response is highly needed to stop further contacts. All correspondence must be by e-mail address above. I will give you tell/ fax numbers where you can contact me when I hear from you. I must use this opportunity to implore you to exercise utmost indulgence to keep this matter extraordinarily confidential whatever your decision while await your prompt response.

NB: Because of the security being mounted on the members of my family, I have decided, that this transaction be kept in utmost secrecy, remember to include your private Tel/fax or mobile number for easy communication.

Best Regards

DR. MRS MARIAM ABACHA

LETTER FROM A CONCERRNED CITIZEN

From: Someone

Sent: Thursday, May 16, 2002 4:02pm

To: Many people

Subject: Beware

I have never been touched like this before since all these 419 nonsense out of our country Nigeria came to my awareness. It's so sad that there is no value for human dignity anymore. Worse still, it is getting out of control.

The night I receive the e-mail (May 10, about 12 midnight), I just returned from a friend's house. He had a call from Nigeria. His sister was on admission at Lagos University Teaching Hospital diagnosed with Typhoid Fever. The doctor in charge had requested that she should have blood transfusion. The doctor asked for the transfusion to be carried out by 11:00pm that night.

The hospital sent her relatives to a blood merchant to go and buy blood. They did accordingly, brought the receipt for the payment to the hospital since they would not be allowed to carry the blood except by hospital staff. The receipt was given to the nurse on duty. Family members kept waiting for blood transfusion to be carried out, nothing happened all night. The patient was unattended to, left suffering in bed for no reason.

The next day, pandemonium struck. No blood transfusion yet. The receipt for the purchase of blood was not available. The nurse was not on dirty. Family members approached the doctor to write another request so they could go and purchase another blood. He refused; they had to wait for the nurse to report to work at night. When she was given the receipt, she did not put it inside the patient's chart. She put it in her bag and went home with it.....while a human being was dying on her bed.

On the 3rd night, the nurse was asked for the receipt, still no blood transfusion which worried family members. The nurse went through bag looking the receipt without finding it. She promised to do something with indignation from confused family members.

When I returned from my friend's house, I read your e-mail. I quickly forwarded it to him with a relief because I told him "I think someone is trying to run a scam on you for money" I am sure that we both went to bed relieved. We decided to investigate whatever the scam was the next days. 6:30am, May 11, it was my friend on the phone sobbing, "Brother Yinka, I just received a call from home, TOYIN DIED OVERNIGHT!"

As if the pain and sorrow is not enough, the hospital refused to release her body to her family. LUTH insisted they would carry out an autopsy.

Toyin's family is a Muslim family. The consultant (sic) to release her body deliberately made herself unavailable while the hospital and the family got into war over the release of her body. Even in death, they violated her religiously (sic) rights.

Searching for rational explanation for all these miseries, I contacted both Nigerian and American Doctors here to educate me on everything that happened. I found out that:

1. The request for the blood transfusion was a scam to make money out of the family

2   The nurse, the doctor and the blood merchant were working together
3   The adamant move to carry out autopsy was an effort to remove body parts for sale.

As much as I appreciate your making us aware of what is going on in Nigeria through your personal experience, we owe it to ourselves to send such information to as many as all the 120 million Nigeria in the world if possible and also to make this a serious issue through the media, the authorities and the elected public official at home, and to let them know that we are measuring their competence based on their responses to public cries.

REACTIONS TO 419 LETTERS

Chima,

I'm sorry to hear what happened to you. The exact same thing (sic) happened to my husband about a year ago. They intercepted a call he made to his uncle and told him the exact (sic) same story his uncle had just been in an accident and needed blood immediately, send $15,000, etc. Luckily for my husband, his aunt who is a registered nurse was with us at the time. She asked the "doctor" some medical questions which he couldn't answer, of course. At that point, we started suspecting foul play. Our fear at the time was that his uncle may have been abducted or something like that, Anyway, What is ended up costing us was a high telephone bill, as we had to call several relatives back home to be sure if this uncle was not in any danger.

It's really a shame that there are number of people in Nigeria who spend so much time thinking of new ways to con people. Every other week at work, we receive faxes from 419 people who claim to b princes, priests, ministers etc in Nigeria You can guess what they are after, money. This is very embarrassing since everyone at work knows that I'm from Nigeria.

Hand in there bro. I know it's it very frustrating, but try no to think about it so much. I know it's easier said then done.

REACTION TO 419 LETTERS

Hello everyone,

Regretfully I fell victim to a new 419 scam yesterday. I lost over $1,000.00 I have decided to share this story with all of you so no else could fall victim to this ill-advised scam. As I was preparing to go to work yesterday, I decided to call my sister at Lagos to say hi and find out how she was doing. My sister was at work so I called her office. When someone answered the phone, I asked to speak to my sister. He asked me where I was calling from and I told him. He told me my sister was involved in terrible car accident and she was being rushed to the hospital. He emphasized the fatality of the accident and gave me the hospital's phone number. I called the hospital immediately and someone picked up the phone and introduced himself as a medical practitioner administering treatment to my sister. He told me my sister lost a lot of blood and was in a very critical condition. He added that my sister was under life support machinery at the moment and he was a doctor. He claimed that my in-law (my sister's husband) has been contacted and was on his way to the hospital, but might be held up in traffic for a while.

At this point, I was scared to death. I told the doctor to do everything in his power to keep my sister live. He told me he needed some money immediately to buy some blood for my sister since she lost so much blood. He told me that blood bank was closing in about an hour and he needed the money immediately to make the reservation. He however, emphasized he was not guaranteeing my sister's survival, but the blood transmission was imperative and definitely the first step to take. Hey guys, I love my sister to death and would do anything to protect her, so I asked the doctor how much he needed.

He told me to send $1,000 via Western Union and call him with the control number. This was happening at about 7:30AM in the morning and the banks were still closed. I could only withdraw $500.00 using ATM.

CHAPTER EIGHT

Personal 419 Encounters at the Airport

A lady who was based in the United States was to visit Nigeria for an official engagement. She was to carry out some duties in Abuja as well as Lagos. I was to coordinate the Lagos angle of her visit which entailed paying courtesy call on the Deputy Governor as well as meeting one of the Commissioners in the State. First I was billed to meet out guest at the airport and take her to one of the big notable hotels in the city. The founder of the NGO which invited the lady to Nigeria in the first case had warned me never to allow any other person(s) to take the lady at the airport, for security reasons. That warning turned out to be our saving grace. While I waited for arrival, my mobile phone rang. The voice on the line was strange, yet he wanted to confirm my identity. The fellow told me he was also at the airport to pick the same lady and that he belongs to an organisation working in the same field. Just about the same time, the lady emerged at the arrival lounge and it was easy for the earlier caller to identify me and the guest. We exchanged pleasantries and I quickly grabbed the guest's luggage. As we walked to the parking lot, I signified we were going to enter my saloon car. The other guy who I later gathered got my phone number from the guest whom he earlier met on the internet had hired a four-wheel-drive-jeep, another vehicle, of friends, possibly for special effects.

I ignored as I ushered the lady into my car and we drove towards the hotel the guy said he had booked for the guest. By the time we got to the hotel, I found that it was not a pleasant place and was in an obscure corner, close to a canal. For security reasons, we declined and I eventually took the lady to a big notable hotel with full security. Before the guy came to meet the guest the following day, we had left the hotel for the day's assignment. The fellow kept bombarding my phone, demanding to known where I have taken the visitor and raining abuses on me. Naturally, I informed them where we were with Deputy Governor. They broke through the security network and harassed me and the guest at the high table. But they could not get into the vehicle conveying us with the cabinet members. They rained more abuses on me and it was then I began to have inkling they did not have the credentials they claimed to possess.

The lady left Nigeria safely, few days later, resolving to block all contacts with the guy and his group.

A year later, a friend of mine informed me about the existence of a group of deceitful persons in his neighborhood who sent letters overseas in his foreigners into "419 activities", and he had warned them to desist if they did not want the long arm of the law to catch them. That did not make any sense to me until I passed through the neighborhood two months later and I spotted the same guy who had come to the airport intending to pick the lady from U.S.A several months earlier. Few minutes later, I told my friend about the guy and described him Alas, he was the same guy my friend spoke about. Thus, I confirmed that the visiting lady was just lucky not to have fallen into an organised scam.

ELECTRICITY BILL'S 419

In Nigeria, estimated electricity bills are sent out to consumers despite the fact that they have meters installed in their homes. The National Electric Power Authority (NEPA) was known to supply power to irregular periods. Most big cities are in constant blackout. Over 70 percent of the population depends on generators to power their industries, homes and businesses, yet the government owned Electricity Company now called what is PHCN gives people estimated and erratic bills. They called them "crazy bills" and make to fuss about it. The company was enmeshed in a "crazy bill" of N99million, about $700,000 US which was given to Dr. Ayo Macaulay, a medical practitioner at Mushin, Lagos for one-month consumption in a small apartment. The officials refused to adjust the bill for months until the issue was made public in the SUN Newspaper. The organisation later claimed that their meter was reading backwards.

But shouldn't it occur to those who fed the rubbish into a computer that N99 million could not be consumed in a flat. But such cases are used as avenues for extortion. Reaping where someone did not sow is scam-either officially or unofficially. It is believed in some circles that scammers and con artists are creeping into the civil service and using official cover to deceive people and siphon their funds.

An honest consumer could be officially given a "crazy bill" to propel him to negotiate, give bribes or offer incentives. Under this grand design of official deception, you may have your electricity disconnected until you negotiate, re-negotiate, pay officially and unofficially to get connected for an estimated bill you never consumed in the first case.

A school of thought claimed that the scenario has become more terrible under the Power Holding Company which replaced the NEPA

PERSONAL 419 EXPERIENCES WITH INTERNET BANK ACCOUNT

I was a regular contributor of short stories and other creative works to an American story publisher based in Virginia, USA, between 2002 and 2003. My publisher opened an Internet Bank Account for me at an Internet based account and regularly paid my royalties there. After my return to Nigeria, I regularly checked my balance on the Internet hoping it would appreciate to a level that I would now use it to make procurements through the available credit cards. I tried to check my bank balance sometimes in 2005 and discovered it was impossible. I wrote series of letters to bank and got some replies on what to do to reactive my account which they claimed they thought was being accessed by some "foreigners" other than the owner of the account. I followed all the instructions, yet my account was never reactivated. I made several calls to the bank and could not get to talk to any one in particular. At a stage, I got frustrated and gave up. By September

2006, I still could not check my account which had been closed by the bank giving me the impression that I may have lost the money there in. My publisher who paid the money there in the first case wrote series of letters which were ignored. Internet or electronic is prone to fraud from within and outside the country. People's account could be confiscated under spurious claims.

FAKE DRUGS AND 419 DRUGS AND DECEPTION

In September 1990, 102 children died after receiving treatment in seven cottage, and Government hospitals in Ibadan city in Nigeria. After some investigations it was discovered that all deed children had earlier fake paracetamol syrup, which was taken with multivitamins chloroquine, cough syrups. In another case, 24 and of 26 children taken to a hospital died. When analysis of the paracetamol syrup was carried out, it was discovered that a toxic material was present in the paracetamol syrup. One of the raw materials labeled and sold as "propylene glycol" was ethylene glycol, a poisonous material that gives rise to Kidney failure. Investigations by the Federal Minsitry of Health indicated that one company called Delebayo and Co Ltd (Pharmaceutical Division) made procurement from Osigweh Pharm, Chemists Ltd. Uza Street, Onistha. The company fraudulently claimed on the label of the bottle of the toxic substance that it was manufactured by Drugham Trading B.V. industriele and Handle Maatschappy, Almere Haven Holland. Labelling adulterated drugs as genuine ones is a criminal and dangerous thing which has led to the death of several people in Nigeria. Onitsha, Idumota in Lagos and Kano had been known as the haven of adulterated drugs barons impaired the health of many Nigerians. Drug India and China to influence the reduction of the potency of certain drugs and also adulterate some. These went on four years until Ex-President Olusegun Obasanjo government appointed Professor Dora Akunyili as the Director of National Agency of Food and Drug Administration (NAFDAC).

The professor has been able to combat fake drug and barons who not only involved in the manufacture of fake drugs to deceive the public in order to make money falsification of drug labels is nothing but 419 or scam.

According to Dr. Fred Adenika, a renown pharmacist and author of PHARMACY IN NIGERIA, the poisonous "ethylene glycol" used in compounding the paracetamol syrups, which was "falsely labeled" (is also deception or 419) and misbranded as propylene glycol, was obtained from unlicensed freelance vendors in Port Harcourt who sold it to registered chemist's shops in Onitsha and Ikorodu.

According to Adenika they in turn sold it to a government compounding hospital in Jos and a missionary hospital in Ibadan. In the book, Adenika recalls how Dr. N.D. Itudu had in 1988 on studies of 486 street market samples in Onitsha, Lagos, Kaduna and Ibadan. After laboratory analysis, Dr. Itudu found "only 68 percent of the drugs were "normal" 22 percent were "substandard and 4 percent were "dangerous" (meaning they were wrong, contaminated or contain high amount active ingredients. In fact, the country as at that time had promulgated Decree 21 of 1988 to fight Counterfeit and Fake Drugs. The *African Science Monitor* were I once worked as Editor with Dr. Adenika as one of the members of the thirteen-man Editorial Board notes that 9 percent of fake drug in Nigeria were imported from England, 3 percent each from Ireland and India, 2 percent Germany, Italy and Switzerland adding that Nigerians are known to be behind these fraudulent or fake drugs in 419 importations.

The National Agency for Food and Drug Administration and Control (NAFDAC) was set up by a military decree 15 (now an Act) TO "regulate and control importation exportation manufacture, advertisement, distortions, sale and use of food, drugs, cosmetics, medical devices, bottled water and chemical".

FAKE DRUGS AND PRIVATE INVESTIGATIONS

Few years ago, SWIPHA, a pharmaceuticals company affiliated to Roche was concerned about the faking of one of her products. Consumers also complaining about not going the required result from the formulated drug. So SWIPHA management consulted PAHEK SECURITY SERVICE LTD, a private security company which guarded SWIPHA facilities to help in finding out those who were responsible. PAHEK through Mr. Otoo, the General Manager (Investigations) began an extensive private investigation to detect those who were behind the fraudulent and fake drug labeling. Preliminary fake drugs. The man lived and operated in Kano in Northern Nigeria, yet his dangerous activity spread across the country. With the aid of security agents, t he man was nabbed in Kano. When interrogated, the man pleaded that he would divulge the name of the godfather of the fake drug as he was just one of the links. According to him, the godfather lived, operated and controlled the dangerous drug network from Onitsha, the heartland and gateway to the Eastern Region.

The investigators arrested the man who led them to Onitsha where the godfather was picked up and the case was reported to the National Agency for food and Drug Administration control (NAFDAC).

The drug ring was powerful. Each of the arrested men offered government officials who took over the investigation. But they declined.

The culprits were later walking freely on the street. The investigators were stunned. They wrote a petition and complained about what was going on. Somehow, with what can be described as divine intervention, the Federal Government appointed Dr. Dora Akunyili as the Director General of NAFDAC. No one knew who she was. Strangely, the private investigators and other government security agents discovered that few weeks later, the drug cartel they picked at Onitsha was back in detention and prosecuted. They were relieved.

FAKE/QUACKS OR 419 MEDICAL PRACTITIONERS

Quackery in any profession is based on false claims, deception and fraud. Many cases of people claiming to be medical practitioners when they are not could be found in the country. They are mostly in large cities such as Lagos, Ibadan, Kaduna or extremely rural areas where the hand of the law can hardly find them. Many years ago, there was the case of a prominent politician who reportedly brought a Pakistani houseboy who claimed he was a Medical Doctor into Nigeria. He became a very dangerous person. People who became sick in the community were he operated died at an alarming rate. Dr. Martin Akpan a medical doctor based in Uyo, Akwa Ibom, State narrated in The Guardian on Sunday of June 29, 1987 how a teacher (who claimed he had been treating people) infected his own relation with a chemical used in preserving dead bodies) while "treating" her.

He also narrated how a medicine seller ended up circumcising a baby and ended up damaging the organ. I once worked in a Dental Hospital where the office assistant, a messenger was secretly extracting teeth and giving local people dentures without the knowledge of the authorities. He was secretly stacking away dental materials t his house and privately treating people from his observation to everyone the day a woman with an in appropriate denture and swollen mouth traced him to the office which did not return on time.

There was a time I was investigating the use of a new drug for the treatment of river blindness in the early 1990s. I approached one hospital in a suburb of Lagos to get reactions from the Medical Doctor on duty. I was ushered into the office of this medical practitioner in charge of the place. During the interview, I found he had no absolute idea of what river blindness is, not to talk of having heard of the new drug. I then began to educate him, and he later confessed, that he was a physiotherapist and that his wife who was in Saudi Arabia owned the clinic and he was "managing it for her"

"THIS HOUSE IS NOT FOR SALE" SCAM

"This house is not for sale! This is the inscription you will notice on some o the buildings, especially in Lagos, Nigeria. It is an indication that 419 or fraudulent claims on properties exist. Properties papers or even alter genuine ones to dispossess people of their landed properties. In some cases, people's land was taken by force or might. Stories abound that some people could be daring. They jus went to someone's uncompleted building and completely took over the property, sometimes with the connivance of fraudulent government officials. In families where members fought over their father's properties, one or more of the children could decide to sell any of the properties without the approval or consent of other members. In order to prevent people from buying such houses, a sort of italic would be inscribed boldly on the building to deter people from buying. *"This house is not for sale,"* simply means Buyer Beware!

CHAPTER NINE

Academic or Educational 419

Sometime in 2006, a man called a Governor in a state in South Western part of Nigeria during a phone-in programme and told the Governor that he had no job despite the fact that he had a doctorate degree in Engineering. The stunned Governor offered to help and he gave the caller the name of an organisation where he could get a job through him. The caller who was claimed he had a first class honours degree visited the company he had a first class honours degree visited the company with some certificates. When the organisation interviewed him, they found he could not defend any of the certificates he claimed. H later owned up he procured them through a "syndicate" that manufactures and print fake certificates. The Sun Newspaper in Lagos in 2006 carried out extensive investigation on a place called Oluwole in the heart of Lagos. Oluwole is a place globally known to be the centre of fake certificates and documents. Operators of fake documents at Oluwole, out could issue a certificate to the effect that a Nigerian had studied Lion and Elephant Engineering at the University of Moon, in open sky above the earth!

There was a time a Polytechnic Lecturer who claimed he too had a doctorate degree disappeared from the campus. Story has it that he was being investigated when it dawned on the authorities through protests from the students that his teaching was below expectations. He vanished when his certificates were being verified.

There was the case of a man who also met a renowned Educationist at Abeokuta, claiming he too was unable to seek employment with his doctorate degree. The Educationist gave him a letter to seek employment at a University in Ogun State. It was later found out that the fellow had no such certificate. He took to his heels afterwards.

There was a fellow who claimed he was a medical Doctor and he was indeed practicing medicine until the truth was known and he fled. Many people through medical degree have killed several people through their fake practice. All these are based on deception. On another level, some intellectuals simply doctor their findings steal or plagiarized other people's work cleverly. Some are caught while many escape. The story of the Korean who claimed to have made discoveries on HIV only to speak the contrary is very instructive on global academic fraud.

TIPS TO PROTECT YOU FROM GLOBAL SCAM AND NIGERIAN BASED 419

1. Keep your credit card very well and quickly alert the authorities when it is stolen.
2. Protect your bank account number and books very well.
3. Do not let out personal information and details about your family and financial status and expectations.
4. Some desperate con artists peep through documents and other people's personal information.
5. One scam common is advanced countries and incorporated into Nigerian and African system is what is known as the pyramid scheme in which are no products, you people are asked to recruit other into financial programmes which they claim would elevate them up the top of the scale as they bring interested people. Some of these schemes appear genuine. Forms may be printed and circulated. They may even have offices. There was a time some perpetrators of similar schemes in Nigeria even penetrated religious places, but they often vanished into the air after the collapse of such businesses.
6. Some con artist gave fake awards or prize which they claim their victim have own. But you can identify them when they, ask you to pay "processing fees" (which could be a token fee or a huge sum of money) including hotel expenses etc to claim your award or prizes.
7. Some products or drugs are linked to scams.

These products do not contain the necessary ingredients that can con artists claims they have. They may claim to contain ancient secrets or key to breakthroughs. But the claims are fraudulent and the writers smile to the banks while the recipients suffer and lose. Drug used to be faked on a large scale in Nigeria until war was waged against them globally by Nigeria Agency for Food and Drugs Administration (NAFDAC)

8. Beware of letters, cell phone text messages, or e-mail that claim you have own a prize from any organisation you never had any dealings with.

REFERENCES

1. Tunde Akingbade, The 419 Scourge, *Security and Safety Magazine*, Lagos Issues 50, 2003.

2. Securing Banks against Criminals, *Security and Safety Magazine*, Lagos issues 5, 2003 Pg   26

3 Internet Network Security, *Oil Week, Newspaper*, Lagos June 19, 2006 Pg 17

4 Directory of Crimes of Persuasion, USA 2006

5 Patrick Keku and Tunde Akingbade, *Travelers Guide to Living in Nigeria. Security and Travel Tips* Indiana, USA 2003

6 Shell Scam Alert

7 MTN, Nigeria, Scam Alert.

CHAPTER TEN

Contemporary Crimes In Banks and Financial Institutions

Jesse James, American's most notorious armed robber and legendary thief who was believed to be the first to rob a moving train in the USA was asked why he began to target banks and rob them. Jesse, the son of a Baptist Pastor asked his inquisitors, where is money kept? They answered banks! This response demonstrated the main reason why banks are targets of robbers, whether armed or unarmed.

Jesse James whose cave where he used to keep his loot has became a tourist's delight in Missouri robbed the Mid West of USA with ease until he was shot dead by gang members who wanted to draw a ransom of $10,000 placed on his head. Also Bonnie Parker and Clyde Barrow were known to be the greatest bank robbers who left sorrow and blood everywhere they descended in Mid West of the USA. The couple was the greatest terror to banks and individuals in their time. It appears the Mid West of USA and Nigeria's Mid West have some things in common. Parading the most notorious bank robbers! Lawrence Anini and Sunday Osunbor were from the region and they terrorized the people of the State and stole from banks.

America's Mid West and Nigeria's Mid West have both produced gangsters who targeted financial institutional maimed and killed in order to get money out of their vaults. Some of them, like Jesse James and Anini were known to have even thrown stolen money to the populace after each raid.

BANK'S VULNERABILITY AND SECURITY

All over the world, security of banks have been a major concern for operators of these financial houses. Bank security is a specialized area that focuses on protection of both external ad internal facilities risks that many inflict loss on their organisation. Banks in Nigeria became major targets of armed banditry in the early couldn't have been after the war

Today's armed robbers have engaged all kinds of tactics to gain entry into banking halls and vaults. Besides, there are other internal pen robbers who use their knowledge and position within the banks to defraud. These days, bank robberies are done with the connivance of officers within banks. Before we go into some case studies of tactics used by armed robbers we will highlight the vulnerability of banks and financial institutions.

Generally, banks are exposed to certain risks. Some of the risks could be from natural causes or man made. Natural causes could emanate from fire, windstorm, earthquake; tornadoes (in some foreign countries) flood, building collapse (recently in our country). It could be as a result of natural causes or man made through defects in construction processes. The real man-made threats emanates from robbery, kidnapping within and outside bank premises.

INNOVATION IN ROBBERY

SCENE ONE:

A group of armed bandits waited patiently very close to Wema Bank Nigeria Ltd., and CITI Bank in Victoria Island area in Lagos. A customer who was armed with a gun emerged from one of the banks and approached his car. Being a security conscious person, the customer spotted the strange faces of the armed robbers some distance to the banks. He then brought out his gun to confront the robbers. On sighting this blood customer, the robbers were smitten with fear possibly because this customer's huge physique portrayed him as a security man. The bandits entered rushed their gateway car and sped off at once. The customer rushed bank manager. The bank manager who had not had any encounter with the armed robbers did not decipher that he had just been saved from "the valley of the shadow of death" of notorious armed bandits who prowl the streets of Lagos. He shrugged off the claim and settled down to his business of monitoring figures and cash flow behind the bank counters. The worried customer walked out of the bank, too a glance at the adjacent street, entered his car and drove off without any hitch.

Three days later, the robbers returned to the bank and carried out their operation. It was then that it dawned on the victims that the customer was not carrying wolf three days earlier. Unknown to the bankers what the customer who had warded off the armed robbers when they first came was carrying was a toy gun. It was such a big gun that no one would have suspected it was a toy gun and this huge customer had always armed himself with this gun because of the frequency of armed banditry in Lagos.

SCENE TWO

In yet another robbery encounter in a Lagos bank, bandits pretended that their vehicle had broken down near bank. They began to push the vehicle towards the bank giving an indication that they were battling to get the care working. The policemen on duty became furious. They reportedly walked towards the men who were pushing the car near the bank and barked order at them. The men pounced on the policemen, over powered them, and began to operator unhindered.

SCENE THREE

The bank had closed to customers. The whole place was quiet. Some men carried some "Ghana-Must-Go' bags (the symbols of cash movement by the rich in Nigeria) and approached the security men at the bank premises informing them that they wanted to lodge huge sums of money stacked in the "Ghana-Must-Go" bags. The security men believed the story and so, opened the gate to inform the manager of the presence of "important" customers wishing to lodge money. The "very important customers" turned out to be armed robbers. They pounced on the security men and gained entrance to the bank. Of course they had a field day as they operated unhindered. It was later discovered that what they had in the Ghana-Must-Go bags were newspapers.

SCENE FOUR:

The bank had also closed and everyone had left. Security men were on guard to protect and other valuables. One of the colleagues came on a visit. He was armed with assorted mouth watering food and drinks. Few minutes later, the men sat down to eat and drink. They had not gone fell asleep. Some faceless individuals joined the "insides" and operated unhindered in the bank as the security men went into deep sleep.

And very recently, another innovation by some men who flash a law Enforcement-Officers identity card at people who step out of the banking hall. These people are told that they are suspects being trailed by the police following a tip off. At the end of the drama, they are thrown into unmarked vans and driven to places where focus here. We are concerned with how banks are defrauded or robbed and strategies of protecting the banks and financial institutions. Generally, there are certain basic rules and principles that guide banks and finance houses towards effective security. The most import challenge that faces the security personnel in banks and finance houses come from criminal activities which could originate from within the banks itself through careless divulging of information) or external, through desperate and carefully planned attacks from bandits. Security personnel in Nigeria are aware that banks are on the top of the list of organisations that are vulnerable to attacks by armed robbers. In recent times, focus has shifted to petrol too that churches or after the close of sales. Lt me add too that churches are equally becoming targets of robbers especially during the period of harvest when cash donations are involved. Anywhere there is money such as the bank, there is likelihood of robbery. There is no doubt that the bank has a higher appeal to robber all over the world. This is why, for example, in 1968, there was a protection Act of Banks which (1991) was amended in 1991 by the government. The Act initially placed emphasis on devices and equipment that guarantees security of banks. However, the revised version placed emphasis on the procedure brought the issue of security in Banks. The Act registered by the government with deposit institutions Federal Deposits Insurance Corporation and other allied institutions into focus.

More importantly under the revised Act, security officers in charge of banks are required to file reports to the board in charge of administration and implementation of policies on annual basis. This Act, according to observers in the security industry indicates that the security officers are now professionals. In one of the treatises on: Bank Security by *Security and Safety Magazine*, "this change is interpreted by most banks as a reason for appointing qualified security professionals as designated security officers mostly with a background in previous security related positions and/or experience in law enforcement."

There are certain standards that must be met in bank security. Apart from the provision of security devices in banks, the Banks Protection Act (BPA) stipulates that there must be a protected place where cash and other valuables are stored including, an alarm system, illuminating system for the vault and locks that are tamper resistant.

However, despite all these protective guidelines, banks and finances houses have become the target of criminals as have been stated earlier. Apart from armed attacks, banks are now vulnerable because of the electronic or computer age which was meant to facilities easy access to operations.

MODERN TIMES

In the past, banks have been under the threat of burglary, robbery, cheque frauds, and schemes to defraud under the guise of loans, these days, frauds are carried out internally and externally through Electronic Fund Transfer (EFT), Automatic Teller Machine (ATM.) There are also internet Banks in the United States and Europe. It is instructive to note that fraudsters have acquired computer skills and dexterity which enables them to rob without carrying guns. In 2002, Nigeria lost N12.9 billion in 796 fraudulent cases. These are the known or reported cases. Many have probably been swept under the carpet. It is generally known that funds are carried out in

Banks through the opening of accounts with fictitious names and locations. These fraudsters also use fictitious names, locations and identifications on the internet to defraud people across the globe. A cyber criminal may inform a bank or victims that they live in Ivory Coast or Ghana when they are actually resident in Lagos.

FRAUD IN BANKS

Frauds in banks are often carried out through collaboration and connivance between officials and outsiders. In very bizarre cases, unscrupulous officials design and execute internal embezzlement systematically that they are often undetected by their bosses. In some cases, the bosses are the thieves. In these days of evangelism of all kinds of faith, the tight faced, shawl or veil carrying "religious" woman may be financially more dangerous than he woman with shocking assorted lip sticks and boobs-exposing garments. For example a female cashier who was believed to be a religious zealot carefully defrauded a first generation bank in Lagos of N48 million in what was believed to be a carefully scripted plot with a pastor. Of course, the messages and preaching from the tracts she reportedly distributed made no meaning to her as the "devil" pushed her into the fraud. These days, it appears the women are taking over from men in internal bank frauds. There was the case of some married women who allegedly stole Western Union married women for their customers. The police retrieved all kinds of driver's licenses; from the female bankers were immigration officers or road safety marshals. Experts believe that 80 percent of frauds in banks are carried out internally while 20 percent are carried out by outsiders. It believed that banks with large staff and billions of cash are prone to big or large scale frauds.

A study revealed that sharp practices in banks also occur through deposits made in bank tellers. Those who usually defraud banks from within are officers who have won the confidence of their superiors over the years. Dishonest insiders have been able to master the rudiments of electronic fund transfer (EFT), set up fictitious accounts around the world and used same to embezzle. In a particular scenario, an officer who unknown to the authorities used to stuff cash into his person within his own closed cubicle was caught through the CCTV! Dishonest bank officers who are in charge of computer or Electronic Fund Transfer usually stole from lodge organisations in order to conceal their fraud. In the USA, electronic funds transfer frauds are carried. The question now is; how does a security officer play any role in ensuring safety or protection of the bank from electronic fraud when he is not directly inside when the action take place?

At this juncture, I will try to explain some of the tricks generally used to defraud so as to open our eyes in order to individually proffer solutions in our places of work as professionals.

With the introduction and use of internet in the country, cyber crimes have also come into fore. People easily sit behind their computers, steal passwords or assume names and roles, which are fictitious in order to defraud individuals and banks. Today, this is the easiest way to steal globally. Nigerians have been noted worldwide as one of the greatest fraudsters on the Internet. Young men and women claim to be the custodians of millions of dollars wishing to part with a certain percentage.

CYBER CRIME

Cyber Crime is a major threat to banks and financial institutions. Under this, there are various tricks by fraudsters behind the computers to defraud. These tricks which are used to steal from people's saving, inheritance includes; tele marketing fraud, consumer scams on telephones (Known as 419 in Nigeria), so called pyramid schemes in which someone is told that the more people interest or percentage he gets. Others schemes to defraud are; chain letters, various courses and degrees are offered on cyber crime to avail people of the schemes and ploys of internet thieves and criminals. There are also cyber crime lawyers, investigators and forensics especially in advanced countries. Modeling agency, credit card fraud, counterfeit money orders, tax fraud, lotteries, gemstones, mining scams, real estate fraud, vanity press publishing, untrue literary contests, Green card lottery, scholarship, and work at home baits, non-existence scholarship, etc. I carried out an investigation on an extensive pyramid scheme used by an American organisation to take money from innocent Nigerians. The investigation was published by the *Sunday Vanguard* newspaper with global reactions. See full report in the next chapter.

REFERENCES

1. Tunde Akingbade, Securing Banks against Robbers, Security and Safety Magazine, Vol 41 Lagos 2003

2 Tunde Akingbade, Internet Crime, Nigerian Security Journal, Vol1, Lagos, 2007

3. Tunde Lewis, Security and Safety Magazine Vol 51 Lagos 2003

4 Patrick Keku and Tunde Akingbade, Dangerous Days and Savage Nights, Indiana USA 2003

5 Tunde Akingbade, Nigerians Millions Trapped in America, *Sunday Vanguard* Feb. 18, 2007

6 *The Sun* Newspaper, Lagos, Sunday 24th June 2007

CHAPTER ELEVEN

Nigerians' Millions Trapped in America

—I introduced my friends to the business; now we have lost all – Victim

MILLIONS of Naira belonging to some Nigerians are trapped in some financial institutions in the United States. There are fears that the institutions may be out to scam Nigerians using some legal authorities. In some of these cases, the business starts as legitimate until something goes wrong under some claims made by the American companies that they doubt the identity of the Nigerians whose money are lodged in their vaults when they what to withdraw or check their balance. Others hide under what they call an order that prevents them from doing business with countries that engage in money laundering citing Nigeria as one of them. Investigations last week indicate that the Nigerian victims are now trapped in a vortex of poverty and shame. Some have their marriages heading for the rocks while others have suffered psychological inertia and cannot claim their certificates from the authorities because they are believed to have defrauded their colleagues. This reporter, for example, has his money trapped in an America organization on the pretext that internet fraudsters may have pried into the account. Several e-mails and phone calls have not made the organisation to defreeze the account.

The worst scenario is the case of Mr. Emeka Anyanwu, a business administration graduate, who started what would have been a business to take him and his colleagues to the financial fulfillment with an American company Cash Card International. They got messages that they cannot retrieve their money because the US authorities have put Nigeria on the list of countries that are not cooperating on stemming money laundering. Anyanwu spoke with Tunde Akingbade on the issue. All through Monday and Wednesday, last week, Akingbade called Cash Card International in West Indies and Minnesota, USA and later interviewed their representative simply called Eric on the internet. Excepts of both interviews below:

WHAT is your name and what is the problem you are having with the American Cash Card Company?

My name is Emeka Anyanwu, I am from Imo State. There was a time I had an opportunity to do business with Cash Card International Centre based in Minnesota. Actually, it was a referral programme. The idea was that we should bring persons to the business and we will get referral bonuses. At first, we were getting on fine and later we realised that they were trying to be smart by putting on one or two information on the internet which we thought were all scams. In this business I have good reasons to believe that no fewer than four million Nigerians have been ripped off and they are quietly licking their wounds.

The estimate that I have is that what we have lost could be close to one billion naira. Each time we write and press to have our money, all we see is that these people ignore us because we cannot cross the sea to America to fight them one on one to retrieve our money trapped in the Cash Card International account.

How much have you lost, personally? I have an investment of about N980, 000. I was coordinating my team's activity. Most of them were entrusting cash on me. The total investment of my team was about N4 million.

How many people were in your team? There were about 450 people in my team.

How did this whole event start and when? First, they posted their mission and the whole thing they were doing on the internet. It was a referral programme as I said. We read the company's policy, what they have in stock for participants and we started doing business with them. It was a referral business. They trade with you in gold and at the end of every two weeks they put it back in the Cash Card account. It was an idea that every one of us and whoever was interested to participate would commit fund and your fund is being utilized back into the account. And because it was an international money wire transfer, it was difficult for individuals who did not have domiciliary account to get their money converted to account. So, I was spearheading everything and assisting to transfer the money. Some of my colleagues were coming with six, seven or eleven accounts.

So, you can imagine what N16, 000 in seven, or fifteen places will be. People thought they were actually investing their money. But, precisely, on April 28, 2006, they said they held a meeting in South Africa that Nigeria is one of the countries that had been listed for money laundering and, for that reason, our investment and cash have been frozen until further notice. We kept mailing them. It got to a time when they stopped replying us. If we called them, they didn't talk to us anymore.

Who is the managing director of this company? One Steve Renner.

What relationship - personal or official - do you have with him? Normally, I did not have one on one contact with him. But on some occasion I called the official number they put on the net and someone spoke to me. At the time I started, a man used to talk to me.

When did you start the business? We started early February 2006 And by April they started their problem? Precisely, April, May, June, they first blew the news those countries that they will not deal with, countries that have star or asterisk in their names and they will not be doing transaction with them. We felt it was a normal thing. But the following month they froze our account without any notice.

If they were not going to do any business with you, why didn't they return what they have taken from you? Actually, we felt that this was an international organization. We felt that if Americans are saying that they have the FBI, how can these people act like this? We even wrote to FBI.

And what report did you get from the FBI? Nothing. We are now saying if this company actually had an investment with us and the company will no longer be doing business with us, they should return our capital investment. Apart from the capital investment, we have what is called V Cash account, which is E Gold. In Nigeria, this is like a normal bank account. This is where all our earnings are placed.

But if this company will no longer be doing business with us, why will they freeze the account? I have Cash account.

Do you want Nigeria's EFCC to step into it if FBI has not done something since the EFCC has been collaborating with them to retrieve stolen money from Nigeria? Are you saying EFCC should liaise with their US counterparts to get the money taken from Nigeria? That's what we are trying to say especially Nigeria government and most especially FBI in USA. I know the problems I personally faced and encountered as a youth corps member when I was serving in Benin as they almost killed me because they felt I connived with the American company to defraud them.

You also collected money from other National Youth Service Corps members? I collected from corps members in my team, my state director can testify, my zonal director can testify. The corps members in my team were about 150.

What was the basis of your doing it then? We felt we should use part of our allowances and trade with it so that, after the service year, if we cannot get a job, we will have something to fall back on and to be self sufficient and be self employed since jobs are scarce in the country.

What course did you read? I read Business Administration; I graduated from Federal Polytechnic, Ede, Osun State.

How old are you? I am 29 years old.

What are you doing right now? I have no job. I am still to recover from the trauma. As a young man and from the course I read, I was following the successful business activities of renowned people. I trusted this company. I felt that I could build my capital like these great men, Jim Ovia, Robert G Allen, Robert Goyasaki, the American Chinese. I read tips on how they made money and I followed the steps and also recounted to my colleagues.

You read all these things in school? When I was in school and when I was doing NYSC. It was the principle that these great men preached multiple sales of income, Rich Dad Poor Dad by Robert Goyasaki, the first and second book. I used their principle. I didn't know I was dealing with insincere people who took the money in America. The principles of those great men are real and if you follow them, you will make money. But I fell into wrong hands. I know the company has its headquarters in Minnesota. I have their full address, phone, fax numbers, etc. Robert Goyasaki said in his book that there are four kinds of people.

They are a business owner, an employer, an investor or a self-employed person. I said, okay, let me be a business owner; let me see how I can build income in multiple strings. Of course, I have seen people who passed through this way and used the same system, why will my own be different? Is it because I am a black man? Bill Gates, Benford, etc, all made it through this channel. Are they telling us that if they are in Nigeria, these Americans will do this to us? I know of families which almost collapsed as a result of this problem. Some almost went mad. There is a woman in Benin; she had physical cash trapped in the account. She belongs to a different chain from ours.

I am aware that this so-called pyramid scheme in America is suspect? Well, I never knew that. In fact, that was the first internet business I was going into. I am not an economist, I am a writer. But I have been able to trace and identify scams. I have just finished a book titled, Historical Studies in Nigeria 419 and Global Scam. Both in US and here, I know schemes on doubling money should be carefully looked into.

To me, it's a surprise. As a beginner in life, I decided to give it a trial. I felt that it was genuine. I felt I had stood on my own and the 450 people I introduced will be able to stand too.

I won't blame you but trying to give you an insight into scams? In fact, something should be done to help us. Even the US embassy in Nigeria should be able to help us. I have the facts and figures. Let them say I did not operate this account with them. Let them deny that I did not commit money to them.

How did you operate V Cash account? The V Cash account was the account they told us they were using. It's like here in Nigeria, a company tells you they are using a particular bank. That was the company they told us they were paying our earnings into. I think a different company managed it. So, suddenly we did not have access to that company and the account. There was a time they later introduced another business opportunity to us. They told us they wanted to help us retrieve the money trapped in the V-Cash account.

I got the mail but unfortunately I deleted that. They now said that the business is a backyard door to the old V-cash account. I went into the process; I saw my old account but could not withdraw from it. So this is an indication that these people are far from speaking the truth. I suspected scam. If it was true that Financial Action Task Force froze our accounts, how come they now took us through a backdoor to our account? How did they have the ability to take us to the backyard door to our account such that if you are interested, you can withdraw to start to do the new business?

Probably it was bait? Yes. That means if you are not interested in the new business, the former cash is gone. That's for those who have balance in the V-Cash account. What about those who don't have? What about our actual investment?

If they don't want to do business with Nigeria because of money laundering, etc, why are they calling us again into another business? The same Steve Renner that was the managing director of the former company was introduced as the marketing director of the new company. What were the other problems you encountered? When this thing happened, it almost caused me my NYSC discharged certificate.

How?

Because as a corps member, you are not expected to engage in activities outside your primary assignment. But I had discussions with some of our coordinators and told them the post NYSC job opportunities looked bleak and we should find a way of empowering ourselves. I told them they would not have job to give us after the service and I had seen something to benefit other youth corps members. So, I was given the opportunity to involve my colleagues, but when the whole thing blew open, I was accused of defrauding my colleagues. They said I connived with an American company to defraud them.

Before I realised it, my directors had heard about it, they said I broke the code of conduct. They said it was a deliberate attempt to scam members. They said if the money I had from them was running into a million, then I have made something. Some of my colleagues out of anger wanted to mob me. I had to run. Up till now, I have not collected some of my official documents because of the problems this American company put me.

TORIES

Accounts remain frozen until Nigeria is delisted from OFAC —Cash Card International representative

TUNDE AKINGBADE

Posted to the Web: Sunday, February 18, 2007

Sorry, your browser does not support floating frames

IT has been brought to my notice that some cash belonging to some Nigerians have been trapped in your system. I will like you to give me the reasons the cash have not been released to the owners after the discontinuation of the business. When are you likely to start the business? What is actually going on?

The accounts need to remain frozen until Nigeria is delisted from the United States Office of Foreign Asset Control. (OFAC). The OFAC which is a unit of the US Department of the Treasury administers and enforces economic and trade sanctions based on US foreign policy and national security goals against targeted foreign countries, terrorists, international narcotics traffickers, and those engaged in activities related to the proliferation of weapons of mass destruction. OFAC acts under presidential wartime and national emergency powers, as well as authority granted by specific legislation. This is not a report published by cash cards or the banking institutions but is a report that states which countries are financially stable to do international money transactions with. You can Google OFAC for more on this report.

Nigeria needs to be delisted from OFAC and be listed as a cooperative country again. Once this is done, we can present this to our bank stating that Nigeria is no longer on OFAC and if the bank approves the re-opening of transactions, we can then open the exchange again.

The notion those who transacted business with you are having in Nigeria is that your organization is engaged in a scam and that your Nigerian customers have been defrauded. When will it be possible to remove Nigeria from the so-called money laundering list? If it is not done, does it mean that those cash from Nigeria will be trapped till eternity?

Your system and so called decertification have also rendered some poor Africans poorer than before and some of them have their lives on the line because those who were team leaders almost got mobbed. Some marriages are believed to have collapsed and a housewife almost got mad. Some people believe they have been cleverly robbed? Why did Steve Renner form another company as the marketing director?

Due to Nigeria being listed on OFAC, Cash Cards started to look at alternatives for members. During this time, we went into a joint agreement with the affiliate community. The TAC group said they would allow the usage of V-Cash as a form of payment for the enrolment into the community. In turn, Cash Cards would help market the affiliate community to all its members. We believe that the affiliate community not only is a way for members to use their V-Cash credits but all the research into the TAC group indicated that this is a great way for members to make money through the TAC referral program as well as all the knowledge that would be given to help members start making money on the net.

The notion here is that your company has defrauded Nigerians. How do you react to this image if your" members" cannot retrieve their money?

It is an unfortunate situation that has happened and once Nigeria is delisted from OFAC and our bank approves transactions, we can reopen exchange. But as we need to abide by the rule handed down by our bank and the report from OFAC, we need to do this.

What will be your reaction if these Nigerians get the FBI, our own EFCC, and the US embassy informed about their predicament?

That would be their choice. As stated, it was not that Cash Cards wanted to freeze any account But as Nigeria was listed on OFAC and our bank will not do any transactions with Nigeria due to the OFAC listing, we are currently at a place where our hands are tied. We want to reopen Nigeria to the exchange as we value a lot of our Nigerian customers but we are abiding by the rules and regulations handed down that we can not do financial transactions with a non-cooperative country.

There is nothing at this time Cash Cards can do. Once Nigeria is delisted from OFAC and our bank approves transactions, we can reopen exchange again with Nigeria.

OTHER GLOBAL REACTIONS ON THE INTERNET

Is Cash Cards International Simply stealing From Nigerian Account Holders? You Tell Me... (Pt. 1)

By Mark on March 16th, 2007 in *American Chronicle*

Everyone knows Nigeria's bad reputation as the home for a multitude of scams and illegal activity. As you read this post please note I am NOT trying to be the naïve 'good business' some in depth exposure and discussion. Not all the people doing business on the Net from Nigeria are scammers. Over the years I have met some very nice, hard working people living in Nigeria and they don't all deserve to get financially slammed or dumped on because on Steve Renner from Cash Cards knows how to read the FAFT money laundering country list.

Especially now, since June of 2006 the Financial Action Task Force (FATF) decided to remove Nigeria from its list of countries and territories that are non co-operative in the international community's efforts to fight money laundering. There are really NO hopeful options for a Nigerian who has lost their legitimate funds because of the Cash Cards International 'seizure'.

Additionally, if I had solicited and directly participated in the online business with Nigeria for years, then decided to freeze the funds under the premise of AML, I could walk away with a very sizable amount of 'Frozen Funds' assuming no further legal hassles. Does that make it right?

Was this private seizure done within US law or is Cash Cards 'cashing in' on some lesser fortunate people who did nothing wrong?

Cash Card International is a distributor of ATM cards, an exchange agent for e-gold digital gold currency and also operates their own online currency known as V-Cash. They seem to have been around since 2001. The business is run by Steve Renner a successful Internet marketer and entrepreneur.

In June of 2006 Cash Cards gave this notice to the public:

"Effective Immediately, Cash Cards International can no longer do business with persons or businesses from Nigeria. For a number of years the Financial Action Task Force ("FATF") has placed Nigeria on the "Back List" of Non Cooperative countries in the fight against Money Laundering. According to the US State Department, Nigeria is a worldwide hub for money Laundering activity, and is notorious for Financial Fraud Schemes that involve the International Wire Transfer of funds. For more information:

As an international corporation we have been monitoring the progress of Nigeria to meet the requirements to bee taken off the "Black List". Unfortunately, there just hasn't been enough progress (see first reference above) and as such we must now suspend all transactions with individuals or businesses from Nigeria to include freezing all V-Cash accounts opened by Nigerians. At such time that Nigeria meets the criteria to be removed from the "Black List", we will again open up these accounts."

But as a Nigerian client during that time if you called Cash Cards Minnesota office, your conversation was like this, "…..I got one of the support guys, he told me yes, Nigeria has been taken off the list (FAFT) but their banks are still waiting for the proper green light to resume operation." *http:///www.nairaland.com/

Many if not most Nigerians I've heard from since planning this post said they felt that Cash Cards International may simply be scamming them out of their money. They don't understand why they can't get their funds back. I have to also include my opinion which is-why have they kept these funds?

Tunde Akingbade is a reporter in Nigeria and ended up interviewing by telephone many locals who were on the losing end of the Cash Cards seizure. Mr. Akingbade had this to say,

"The estimate that I have is that what we have lost could be close to one billion naira. Each time we write and press to have our money, all we see is that these people ignore us because we cannot cross the sea to America to fight them one on one to retrieve our money trapped in the Cash Card International account."

Mr. Emeka Anyanwu was interviewed and he is a business administration graduate, with 450 people in his marketing team participating in the Cash Cards referral program:

I have an investment of about N980, 000. [$7,644 USD] I was coordinating my team's activity. Most of them were entrusting on me. The total investment of my team was about N4 million [$31,200]. ….it was a referral business. They trade with you in gold and at the end of every two weeks they put it back in the Cash Card account…. But, precisely, on April 28, 2006, they said they held a meeting in South Africa that Nigeria is one of the countries that had been listed for money laundering and, for that reason, our investment and cash have been frozen until further notice. We kept mailing them. It got to time when they stopped replying us. If we called them, they didn't talk to us anymore.

Mr. Akingbade asks him, "When did you start the business?"

We started early February 2006 …April, May, June, they first blew the news that countries that have star or asterisk in their names and they will not be doing transaction with them.

We felt it was a normal thing. But the following month they froze our account without any notice….We even wrote to FBI.

And what report did you get from FBI?

Nothing. We are now saying if this company actually had an investment with us and the company will no longer be doing business with us, they should return our capital investment. Apart from the capital investment, we have what is called V Cash account, which is E-Gold. In Nigeria, this is like a normal bank account. This is where all our earnings are placed. But if this company will no longer be doing business with us, why will they freeze the account?

This story was originally posted by Tunde Akingbade, February 18, 2007 in the Vanguard

Part 2: Is Cash Cards Simply Stealing From Nigerian Account Holders? You Tell Me…..cash U Partners with Ukash for European Expansion Office Prepaid Solutions-The Ultimate in Online Account Funding

POSTED IN: Online Prepaid Cards, Virtual Currency, International, Debit Cards Withdrawals, e-gold, Digital Gold Currency

4 opinions for Is Cash Cards International Simply Stealing from Nigerian Account Holders? You Tell Me… (Pt 1)

Seun Osewa

Mar 16, 2007 at 3:47 pm The way Nigerians are treated on the Internet is really sad, especially those of us who want to conduct legitimate business.

Cash cards, release the money of Nigerians – Oluniyi David Ajao Mar 17, 2007 at 2:44am

OTHER REACTION TO THE INVESTIGATION

1. Thanks a lot for your articles. I have a strong feeling that somebody it trying to get their own back. Nigeria has managed to build up an extremely bad reputation in money matters. I myself have received dozens of offers to park money on my account and it is well known that quite a number of people, including Berliners, have been stripped of all their assets by Nigerian gangs.

It is also lamentable that the Nigerian government has not taken adequate measures against money laundering, in spite of the assurances of President Obasanjo, who is often enough appearing at Transparency International (IT) meetings. Of course people are Suspicious that too many members of that government might have vested interest in money laundering and therefore refuse to take division action.

This does not exclude that there are enough American crooks that are cheating people. I very much hope that you have not fallen victim to them.

Peter Prufert, from Berlin

2. Tunde, thanks for forwarding the article you wrote. I haven't of this particular scam here, but I know of Americans who fall for similar Pyramid schemes. I really don't have a lot of sympathy for Americans who fall for making money without doing anything…. maybe the pressure in Nigeria are so much greater. Nothing for nothing. I don't play the lottery either….But if a whole group of people, "investors" are being ripped off then something should be done.

Pyramid schemes and chains should be avoided…..have a great day,

Nicole Peskin, New York

3. This is serious and dangerous problem. Walter, USA

Contemporary 419 Letters

The writer of this letter claimed it originated from Togo. Sadly, the name of a renowned film maker was used as a conduct.

FIRST LETTER

Dear Friend,

I am the above mentioned from Kara in the Federal Republic of Togo; I am married to Dr. T…..B…..who worked with GERMANY EMBASSY in Togo for nine years before he died in the year 2004. We were married for Eleven years without a child, (sic) He died after a brief illness that lasted for only four days.

Since his death, I decided not to re-marry or get a child outside my matrimonial home, which the HOLY BOOK is against, when my late husband was alive, he deposited the sum of $ 5,6000,000 – Five Million Six Hundred Thousand United States Dollars, with a reserve/Security Company.

Recently, my doctor told me that I would not last for the next five months due to my cancer problem.

Though what distributed me most is my stroke. Having known my critical condition, I decided to donate this fund to an Organization or better still a God fearing individual that will utilize this money the way I am going to instruct here. I want a fellow that will use this fund on, Orphanage and Widows, propagating the word of God and ensure that the house of God is maintained, the Holy book made us to understand that blessed is the hand that giveth, I took this decision because I don't have any child that will inherit this money and my husband relatives are not God fearing people and I don't want my husband hard earned money to be mis-used by unbelievers. (sic) I don't want a situation where this money will be used in ungodly manner. Hence the reason for taking this bold decision.

I am not afraid of death hence I know where I am going, I know that I am going to be in the Bossom (sic) of the Lord, EXODUS; 14 VS 14 says that the Lord will fight my case and I shall held my peace, I don't need any telephone communication in this regards because of my health also because of the presence of my husband's relatives around me always.

I don't want them to know about this development; with God will things are possible. As soon as I receive your reply, I will forward your personal information's/contacts (sic) to my Lawyer so that he will start processing of the Legal Documents that will make you to be able to make claim the funds before transferring the funds into your nominated bank account your country.

I will also issue you a Letter of Authority that will empower you as the original-beneficiary of the funds. I want you and your family to always pray for me because God has been so good to me. My happiness is that I lived a worthy life as a God fearing person.

Whoever that wants to serve the Lord, must serve him in spirit and truth. Please always be prayerful all though your life.

Please assure me that you will act accordingly as I stated here in. Once I hear from you, I will give to you a Lawyer that I have contacted to take care of this transaction, I will also provide the lawyer personal contact info for you to get in with him and know what is required of you, as to be able to do the needful.

Hoping to hear from you as soon as possible.
GOD BLESS.
My very best regards.
Mrs. Angela TB

SECOND LETTER

Dear Liberty Post: I have been requested by the Nigerian Global Warming Council to contact you for assistance in resolving this matter. The Nigerian Global Warming Council has recently concluded that global warming is worldwide crisis and has procured moneys equaling US$40,000,000. The Global Warming Council is desirous transfer these funds to other parts of the world to fight this problem; however, because of certain regulations of the Nigerian Government, it is unable to move these funds to another region. Your assistance is requested as a non-Nigerian citizen to assist the Nigerian Global Warming Council, and also the Central Bank of Nigeria, in moving these funds out of Nigeria. If the funds can be transferred to your name, in your United States account, then you can forward the fund as directed by the Nigerian Global Warming Council. In exchange for your accommodating services, the Global Warming Council would agree to allow you to retain 10% or US$4 million of this amount. However, to be a legitimate transferee of these moneys (sic) according to Nigerian law, you must presently be a depositor at least US$100,000 in a Nigerian bank which is regulated by the Central Bank of Nigerian. I it will be possible for you to assist us, we would be most grateful. We suggest that you meet with us in person in Lagos, and that during your visit I introduce you to the representatives of the Nigerian Global Warming Council, as well as with certain officials of the Central Bank of Nigeria. Please call me at your earliest convenience at…..Time is of the essence in this matter; very quickly the Nigerian Government will realize that the Central Bank is maintaining this amount on deposit, and attempt to levy certain depository taxes on it, boilerplate posted on 2007-07-02 09:59:58 ET

This letter was sent by someone who used my article in the Sunday Vanguard following an interview I had with one of those who attended the Climate initiative of Bill Clinton in New York. It is full of deception and illegalities. It was however detected.

OTHER BOOKS BY TUNDE AKINGBADE

1. The Wizards who flew into American
   ISBN-1-4107-9622-1(e book)
   ISBN-1-14107-9621-3(paper back)

2. NIGERIA: On the Trail of the Environment
   ISBN 978-31493-0-X

3. DEEP INSIDE GERMANY: Reflection of an Africa
   ISBN 978-34719-1-0

4. ILARO: Memories of Operation "Wet E" and the Civil War Years
   ISBN 978-34719-0-2

5. Famished King, and the Mystery Head
   ISBN 978-34719-0-2

6. All Men Are Devils and other Stories
   ISBN 978-34719-3-7

7. Shuttle from Wasteland: Political and Environmental Imbalance between Africa and USA
   ISBN 978-31493-2-7

8. Forgotten African Stories

CO-EDITED BOOKS

1. Dangerous Days and Savage Nights – Countering the Menace
    of Armed Robbery Nigeria.

    ISBN 1-4107-9910-8 (e-book)

    ISBN 1-4107-9900-X (Paper back)

2. Travelers Guide Living in Nigeria Security and Travel Tips.

    ISBN 1-4140-0627-6 (e-book)

    ISBN 1-4140-0628-4(Paper back)

3. Industrial Security and Practice in Nigeria – Challenges and
    Prospects for the 21st Century

    ISBN 1-4107-9857-7(e book)

    ISBN 1-4107-9858 (Paper back)

*To order send an email to: tintune2003@yahoo.com or text only to
08082419172.*

ABOUT THE AUTHOR

Tunde Akingbade is a distinguished Nigerian environment journalist and playwright. Author of many books, Akingbade won many international award including Vermont Studio Centre, USA, Artists Angel Award in 2001. He is also the Nigerian Media Merit Award winner of Segun Osoba Prize for Journalist of the Year 1992.

He won the United States' Young African Leaders, Award in 1993.

A man of many parts, the author is an actor, a painter and photographer. Akingbade was former Editor, *African Science Monitor* published by African Concord. He worked at *The Guardian and Sketch.* He was a correspondent and one-time freelance USA correspondent of the *Daily Independent* newspaper. He has also writes for *the* **Sunday Vanguard newspaper** in Lagos. He has written for reputable academic journals at the Massachusetts Institute of Technology, MIT, USA and the Netherlands. He is also a Trustee of various NGO'S including International Institute of Professional Security.

The author is the originator of *Our Environment* programme aired on the NTA Network.

He has attended United Nations Climate Change Conferences (UNFCC) and Desertification Convention in Bonn, Germany. The Hague, The Netherlands and New Delhi, India. His works have been presented at Free University, Berlin, European Union of Science Journalists, Budapest, Hungary, British Voluntary Service Overseas (VSO), British Council, Nigeria, Heinrich Boll Foundation Friedrich Ebert Foundation and University of North Carolina at Charlotte USA functions in 2005. The author is a regular commentator on various television and radio stations such as the Nigerian Television Authority, Minaj Broadcast International, (MBI), African Independent Television (AIT) and British Broadcasting Corporation (BBC).

ABOUT THE BOOK

...Chief Segun Olusola, Nigeria's former Ambassador to Ethiopia and creator of the Village Headmaster programme.

The first thing I asked the author was; what made you to write this book? The effort of the author is laudable and it's a trail blazer. This is a very unique book that should be circulated widely through out the country to read among others, secondary and tertiary institutions, employers of labor, National and State Assemblies, Judiciary, Presidency, Federal and State Ministries, Nigeria Police Force, Nigeria Customs Service, Economic and Financial Crimes Commission, ICPC among others.

...Professor Dora Akunyili, Director General, NAFDAC.

Trafficking in-fake drugs is one of the greatest atrocities of our time by a group of people who should not be considered as normal human beings. Europe and America did not teach the people of Nigeria how to fight corruption. Corruption was a tattoo in various parts of the country before the emergence to British Colonialism. In Ibo land, for example, a thief was ostracized even for stealing a fowl. The act of 419 involves two to succeed. What is 419? A criminal outsmarting the other. It is a game of two criminals.

... Evangelist (Dr) Ebenezer Obey-Fabiyi, Juju music superstar

The author's effort is commendable. This is a good book that one needs to read.

...Rasheed Owolabi Taiwo, Comptroller of Customs, Federal Operations Unit, Nigeria

This is a very good book. I am not surprised that it's written by Tunde Akingbade

The Sunday Vanguard Newspaper

The handbook also takes a quick look at the various ways in which the crime of 419 can be eradicated in the country. It provides tips on how to avoid being defrauded on the internet, containing equally the samples of 419 letters as well as testimonies of those who have fallen victims of the dare devils antics.

...The Sun Newspaper

The author commends efforts of Economic and Financial Crimes Commission (EFCC) for working tirelessly to rid the polity of corrupt individuals and recover stolen money. He also commends National Agency for Food and Drug Administration and Control. In all, the book is quite interesting to read as it documents vital issues which everyone should know about deception and fraud.

The Business Eye Magazine

The book also traces the origins of internet usage in Nigeria and the beginning of cyber-crimes. It also detailed the mode of operation of the scammers and those who are susceptible to the crime. The author went to great lengths to give instances of how cash and other hard earned valuables are lost to fraudsters through various means to deceptions.

...Tony Ofoyetan, LLM, BL, FIIPS, Director General, International Institute of Professional Security.

I have known Akingbade running to a decade now as a researcher, investigator and a well traveled person. I am therefore not surprised at his in-depth knowledge of national and international vices that have bedeviled this nation and its honest populace for more than three decades. The author x-rayed internet crime from Nigeria to America, Europe and other parts of the world with practical life.

www.ingramcontent.com/pod-product-compliance
Lightning Source LLC
Chambersburg PA
CBHW020257290526
45784CB00003B/1273